Born in Toronto in 1964, Jocelyn was brought to South Wales at the age of three and grew up in the industrial town of Port Talbot.

She is a full-time carer, artist and jewellery-maker. Jocelyn has had several solo shows and exhibits her art regularly. Her work has been commissioned for publications and theatre. She has been featured in the *Artist & Illustrators* magazine.

Jocelyn's caring role looking after her disabled husband and daughter led her to win a National Carers Award in 2014.

She also has a son and two grandsons. Her passionate empathy towards carers and their roles has resulted in her being invited to sit on the advisory board for Carers Wales.

Throughout her life journey, Jocelyn has used her intuition as a means of support and creativity.

To my mother and grandmother, thank you for the love.

Jocelyn Prosser

SOUL DIVINING

An Intuitional Journey

AUSTIN MACAULEY PUBLISHERS™

LONDON • CAMBRIDGE • NEW YORK • SHARJAH

A CIP catalogue record for this title is available from the British Library.

ISBN 9781528905091 (Paperback)
ISBN 9781528957892 (ePub e-book)

www.austinmacauley.com

First Published (2019)
Austin Macauley Publishers Ltd
25 Canada Square
Canary Wharf
London
E14 5LQ

The sun is shining. It's autumn. I glance at the large ornamental Buddha in the corner of the garden. The last shaft of sunlight will fall on this to end another day. I look at Amy's smiling face. In my mind, there is much to ponder. *Why do we exist? Do we have a mission?* Possibly – but there are no definite answers to these questions. Some things remain a mystery to us. But I do feel, not just in the physical sense. I contemplate my existence and of where I am in the universe – life and its mind-boggling array of problems and pleasures which are all part of the journey. We deal with life on a day-to-day basis, taking in information, processing it and acting on it. My mind has never been the most logical, but I believe the universe can help answer our problems – using intuition. The consequences of life when intuition is embraced or ignored can be life-changing.

I was born in 1964 in Toronto, Canada. My mother was Welsh, my father French. Having studied at Toronto University, my mother had gained a diploma in art. She was the most amazing artist. Even now, I look at her work and still find it so dynamic and fresh. My father was some years older than my mother and owned property in Toronto. He had also served in the French Foreign Legion. Originally, he had come from a small town in central France called Loudun. Having married, the pair bought a house in Toronto. The photos I have seen of it looked sweet and idyllic – unlike life. At the age of three, my mother brought me back to her hometown of Port Talbot in Wales following the breakup of their marriage. My father never kept in contact and would remain a complete mystery to me for most of life.

As a child, I enjoyed my own company and had a great love of animals, a passion that remains to this day. Once, I remember seeing some teenage boys throwing rocks down a slide in my local park. When I approached, I could see a small frog at the bottom of the slide. I just couldn't understand how a person could actually enjoy hurting a defenceless animal. I edged nearer and managed to pick up the frog; thankfully, it was still alive. I ran as fast as I could until I reached my house and hid my new friend in the garden. This incident has stayed with me a lifetime and illustrates that bullies come in all shapes and sizes.

My mother, Mair, had been diagnosed with schizophrenia before my birth. She would sometimes be delusional and manic and was sectioned regularly. To add to this, she had a progressive and congenital inoperable heart condition. Between the two illnesses, she suffered terribly. She was a beautiful, articulate woman – ahead of her time. I remember her hands, such beautiful hands, and the nicotine stain on her index finger.

At teatime, I would return home from school and determine what frame of mind my mother was in. It would take two minutes to gauge her mood. I called this 'happy mammy' or 'unhappy mammy'. If the latter, I would grab a quick sandwich and disappear to the local park until bedtime. I think I became hyper-sensitised to her moods; possibly, this was my first survival tool.

At the age of seven, I learnt to ride my first bike, falling off and getting back on. During my struggle, I had my first migraine; the coloured patterns seemed so magical. Scintillating zigzags and blindspots would affect my vision at times, but I never questioned what it was or told my mother. Occasionally, there would be a pounding headache, it would be another ten years before I would have a diagnosis of migraine.

On occasions I would paint and draw alongside my mother, and this would be the happiest time spent with her. I would love to mix colours and did so many sketches of my little dog, Peppy.

When I was eight, I went on a school trip to London. I can remember buying Peppy a little dogtag as a gift. Returning home, I couldn't wait to present Peppy with the gift I had bought her but it wasn't long before my excitement turned to tears. My mother and gran explained that the dog had had to go. I couldn't understand what they meant, I just kept asking to see my beloved dog. Peppy was gone. I was inconsolable. They wouldn't or couldn't tell me where she had gone but I sensed that it was not good. I have never got over the loss of Peppy and recently I visited my Aunt June who is the last living relative who could tell me what happened to Peppy. All the years I had had the opportunity to ask my gran, I never did for fear of what I would be told. I sat with my aunt awhile and brought up the subject of Peppy.

"I will tell what happened to Peppy if you want me to," she whispered, but I looked at her and knew that it would be upsetting. I didn't want to feel angry at my mother and gran all these years later. I declined. Some things are best left unsaid. All I can say is that Peppy was my dearest, constant friend in what was at times a very unstable home.

Life was very difficult at times, our home was so antiquated and without an indoor toilet or bathroom, the situation became so difficult for my mother, as her health failed. She would struggle to walk to the toilet at the bottom of the garden and I would bathe in front of the fire in a plastic bath. Bare floorboards and damp patches on the walls added to the scenery. I remember my mother painting the piano in the parlour with white paint in one of the delusional moods…it looked so unique and beautiful, like her. All this seemed so normal at the time. Power cuts and candles were also common features of life in the '70s. Somehow now I look back at this era with warm nostalgia, even though the winters could be cuttingly cold in a house with one gas fire, it was home. Clichéd but true, my mother's love kept me warm.

I found it difficult to watch my mother struggling to do things but her strength was ebbing now and she had become so frail. Her soul so weary, she had an awareness of what was happening to her. I hated her suffering so much and just couldn't understand why she had been given this burden in her life. But her dignity was inspiring. She could no longer navigate the stairs, as she was so weak, so our beds were moved downstairs into the parlour. My gran had bought my now-bedridden mother a little handheld brass bell in the shape of a woman to ring if she needed anything. My role was now to care for my mother.

My Aunt June was a great friend to my mum, supporting my mum through mental breakdowns and was a loyal companion despite my mother being quite antisocial on times. My mother loved June dearly.

My maternal grandparents lived a street away but my mother did not get on with my grandfather – a family feud. My gran, who was called Sal, tried to be as supportive as she could, but her resources were limited, as she was a carer for my grandfather, who was blind and had emphysema. I loved my gran so much, a large woman with a wonderful embrace. Her hugs were wonderful. I just felt so safe and loved when she hugged me.

Every day I would see the anguish in my gran's eyes as my mother's health deteriorated. She would say: "Jocelyn, your mother is very ill. One day she won't be here, love." She totally prepared me for my mother's death. Perhaps, I was over-prepared, as every time my mother was taken to the hospital, I thought it would be the last time I would see her. I think back to my gran in awe of her bravery, how hard it must have been to see her child suffering. I know she stayed strong for me.

My first experience of intuition came in the form of a dream. At the age of eight, I had two friends. We would play together regularly, particularly during school holidays. One night I awoke really upset because my dream had revealed my two friends going on a trip without asking me. It was such a vivid dream. The following day, I went to call one of the friends and was told by a neighbour that she had gone on a trip for the day. I then went to call my other friend and her mum told me she'd gone on a trip to Longleat with the other friend. This was my first taste of duplicity and intuition. The feeling of betrayal stayed with me for a very long time.

My mother passed away on July 20, 1975, at the age of 41. I was 11. I felt a sense of relief for her – she truly suffered. My gran had a short quote written into the book of remembrance at the crematorium where my mother's ashes were interred. It said: "Peace after pain, rest off the weariness, safe in God's hands." I found these words comforting. I couldn't quite believe that I would not see her again, but at the same time I felt that she was near me.

After my mother's death, my aunt and uncle decided to take me on a six-week trip to Toronto, Canada, just to help me get over my grief. I loved my Aunt Carrie, who was my gran's sister, and Uncle Will, they were always so kind to me. I loved to visit them, as I would always get a glass of dandelion and burdock pop and chocolate. They both had such a great sense of fun for life, which helped lift my spirits. Grief is such a complicated process, it has so many layers, relief, sadness, anger, longing.

We stayed with my Aunt Iris, my gran's youngest sister. She had emigrated to Canada some years previously and had married Don, a Canadian. They lived and raised their family in Toronto. My mother had also lived with Aunt Iris for a few years before she met my father, so they had been more like sisters. The trip was so enjoyable, meeting cousins and sightseeing. Everyone I met made me feel so welcome and comfortable and it was just lovely to be at my birthplace, it just felt right to be there at this time. Canada is such a beautiful country, so clean, and the people so friendly and passive.

I remember one day I had gone for a walk with my uncle to a local store. As I stood and waited for my uncle to be served, my mind started to gravitate to a magazine rack near the counter. One particular magazine kept drawing my eyes to it. I was compelled to walk over and pick it up – it was a word search puzzle book. Opening the book to the first puzzle, which was entitled 'Steel Companies of the World', the name *Port Talbot* stood out amongst all the other names. What were the chances of finding my hometown in a word search book across the other side of the Atlantic? A warm feeling filled my soul. Something had guided me to the bookstand. I knew it.

My uncle bought the book for me and the story entertained everyone when we got back to my aunt's house. But the feeling I had about the book was more than just coincidence – I had felt the need to pick it up.

The six weeks passed quickly and then it was time to go home. I was missing my mother so much, but I had to face the fact that she was gone. When I arrived home at Port Talbot, I had a lovely welcome from my grandparents, aunts, uncles and cousins. One of the bedrooms had been redecorated in my grandparents' house, huge purple floral wallpaper as I remember, also a brand-new Alba record player. This was now my home.

In my teens, the migraines become more frequent, but there were other symptoms. Visual distortions, seeing people close up, then far away – similar to the action of a zoom-in lens of a camera. I later found out this was called 'Alice in Wonderland' syndrome. Also, strong feelings of *dèjá vu*, which would fascinate me but leave me feeling flat and empty. School was not my favourite venue, but I did enjoy art. Rock music was a passion and my close friend Sue and I loved to go to concerts. I had a few good close friends who helped me tremendously and we have kept in touch all of these years.

Vivid dreams would punctuate these years. One night I dreamt that my close friend Kathy was on a hospital trolley, being rushed to an operating theatre. I woke up startled; my heart beating like a drum, I knew there was something real about my dream. I had been friends with Kathy since we had started school together at the age of five. We also shared the same birthdate, we were and are still soul sisters.

Panicking, I rang her home early that morning. I felt uneasy. Her dad answered the phone. He sounded upset as he explained that she had been rushed to the hospital in the middle of the night.

She had had surgery for a strangulated ovarian cyst called torsion and also had her appendix removed. Luckily, she was now in recovery but there was no doubt she'd been extremely ill. Somehow I knew that she had been in danger, but I just couldn't rationalise the awful dream and how vivid it was. I just knew that it had meant something.

My mind became open after these experiences, with the possibilities that my dreams and feelings were more than just coincidences. *But how does this work?* I would ask myself many times. I've always felt that being open-minded was the right option, not to dismiss or draw a line through my experiences because I didn't understand it. In the vastness of the universe, we understand very little.

At the age of 17, my grandfather passed away. My gran put on a brave face to cover her grief, but I knew that inside she was heartbroken. After this, I decided to opt out of A-level art study; I found the art course boring with the emphasis placed on the history of art rather than practical work. My concentration levels were poor, so revising facts and dates didn't come naturally.

Money was tight but my gran always kept a quiet dignity and never showed me her financial struggle. So I was thrilled when I got a job in the local benefit office which meant that I could help with her finances, just to repay some of the kindness she had shown me. The little bit of money she would have in spare would be spent in the bingo hall once a week. She loved her bingo. On the occasions that she won, she would always buy me a treat of some sort, but never for herself. That's the way she was.

***

I met Darran in 1981 at a local nightclub. He had jet-black hair and big blue eyes. I was smitten at first sight after seeing this tall, dark and handsome man. There was a feeling that I had met him somewhere before. My soul recognised him. After a few years of courtship, I became pregnant. We decided to buy a little house in a small village called Briton Ferry. I had been drawn to a little end of terraced house which Darran and I had viewed twice. When we moved into it, we found out it had been a chip shop called *Jocelyn's* many years ago. We were amazed. Looking forward to the birth of our first child, it was a new beginning. Little did we know that we were embarking on a long, tough journey together.

The pregnancy was very hard, I had a lot of sickness and felt weak all the time. I wondered why I was finding it so incredibly difficult. Were all pregnancies like this, I wondered. Somewhere in my heart, I knew that something was not right, instinct.

Amy was born on Thursday, May 24, 1984, by normal delivery. I remember hearing Howard Jones singing the song 'Pearl in the Shell' on Top of the Pops just before Amy was born weighing 4lb 14oz. Her skin was very red and sore. I was only allowed to hold her for a brief time, as the doctor explained that he had contacted a dermatologist to examine Amy's skin. Darran and I instantly fell in love with this tiny little person, although I was afraid to pick her up. Darran was quick to name her Amy, and I gave her the middle name Sarah, after my gran. Feeling tired and overwhelmed, I just wondered why her skin was so inflamed.

A skin specialist was brought in from Cardiff hospital to examine Amy. After the examination, she was diagnosed as having 'collodion' skin but no explanation or other information was given, the specialist was at a loss to explain what had caused her condition. Sometimes if a baby is overdue, it can develop red skin condition, but Amy was not overdue at all. She remained in the special care child unit for a week and was bathed in olive oil twice daily.

The bathing in oil continued for several weeks after we brought Amy home. She was a month old when she had her first proper water bath. It was upsetting to see her skin so red and angry, Amy just seemed different. Her little elfin face was angelic, always full of smiles, bless her. After some months, she was referred to a paediatrician, as her development was slow. The consultant was quite vague about Amy's skin and slow growth, but Amy was still the most pleasant and sweet baby. As time passed, she had regular appointments with the paediatrician but by now she was suffering lots of infections.

Being so small, she reminded me of a delicate little butterfly. I'd noticed that Amy's hair would grow to a certain length and would then snap off at the roots. She would lose a full head of hair in two days. We later found out this was called 'spontaneous fracture'.

I kept taking Amy back to the GP surgery, just trying to get an opinion about her poor immune system. She had been hospitalised several times for chest infections, water infections and sickness. I was assessed as an overanxious mother, but all the time I kept asking questions that nobody had answers to. It was so frustrating. Somehow I knew there was something wrong.

Darran worked for British Steel at this time. He was a qualified fitter but due to cutbacks, he had been given a labourer's job. He really missed "working on the tools", as he put it. Every year the steel company would shut down for maintenance work to be carried out. This was called the 'stop fortnight'. For these two weeks, Darran would normally have been on his holidays, but he was told that the contractor who was employing men to do maintenance work was looking for qualified fitters. Darran jumped at the chance. Great money and he would be using the skills he had learned during his four-year apprenticeship. This meant he was actually looking forward to working his holidays.

Darran got home after his first day of contract work and talked so enthusiastically about his day and the camaraderie between the groups of men. I loved to see the glint in Darran's eyes when he talked about his work. A men's man, he would delight in workmate banter. My gran would often tell me that I should get up in the early hours of the morning and see Darran off to work, this was because my gran came from an era of women who did this for their men…I had other ideas!

On August 9, 1987, I went to bed with Darran, the following day would be the last day of work for the contractor. Darran had really enjoyed working that week and we had talked about what we would use the extra money for – bills, mortgage and possibly a treat or two. Having a mortgage and one wage was a struggle at times. I had always planned to work full time once Amy was in school, but because of her health, I had to postpone the idea.

That night I had the most harrowing dream. I dreamt I was sitting on my mother's lap as a little girl. She was towering over me and I was crying so much. She kept rocking me back and forth, saying that everything would be all right. Sobbing, I remember her embrace and her voice trying to reassure me. It was the most powerful dream I ever had. Shaking, I woke up and cried uncontrollably. The dream had shaken me to my very core. It just felt so very real. To have felt my mother and hear her voice was overwhelming. I felt that this dream must have some meaning. But I didn't know what.

The following morning, I got up with Darran for the first time ever, gave him a kiss and watched him walk up the street. He had such a distinctive walk, a spring in his step, almost dancing. As I watched him, I felt a deep uneasiness that I had never felt before.

I had arranged to meet Darran at my gran's house in Taibach, Port Talbot, which was near to the steelworks. Darran was due to finish work at 4 pm but had decided to work on just a little longer. It would only take him 15 minutes to walk to my gran's.

Amy was playing happily with her toys when I heard the first siren. I went cold. Then another siren, followed by so many sirens, I felt so agitated. Darran was now half an hour late. I just knew there was something wrong. Every hair on my body stood on end, the feeling is so difficult to explain. I kept pacing around the living room as my gran tried to reassure me. But I knew, I just knew there was something wrong.

Suddenly, the doorbell rang. I felt panic as I opened the door. Darran's father stood there and his mother was beside him. They had divorced many years before. "Darran has been involved in an accident, Jocelyn. You have to come to the hospital with us." His father looked worried. Trying to absorb the situation, I felt too frightened to ask any questions as we travelled in silence.

I really can't remember the journey to the hospital, it was all a blur. Upon arriving at Neath General Accident and Emergency unit, we were ushered into a room. A doctor explained that Darran had been seriously injured. He had lost his left arm in the accident, but now they were doing their best to save his left leg. It felt surreal. Shock, disbelief. I just felt detached. All this information was impossible to take in. I felt I was in some awful nightmare, I convinced myself I was going to wake up.

The police came to explain what had happened. Darran and his work colleagues were working in an area which housed a huge piece of machinery responsible for moving steel rollers. Without any warning, seven tonnes of metal fell. It killed two men instantly and caught Darran on his left side. If it had fallen another foot further, Darran would have been killed outright. It was impossible to take in this type of information. Everything seemed unreal. I kept asking, *Why? Why? Why did this happen?*

For the next few weeks, Darran fought for his life. As gangrene set into his left leg, there was also a problem with uncontrolled bleeding where his femur had come out through the back of his thigh. There was no chance of saving it now, so we were told it would have to be amputated. Darran had to fight for his life yet again during the surgery to amputate his leg. Low haemoglobin levels and infection seemed to have sealed his fate, and the surgeon had prepared us for the worst, but somewhere in me I knew he would pull through. I told him that he had to, through my veil of tears, before he went for surgery. After several hours of waiting, we were told the operation was a success and that infection now was under control. A roller coaster of emotions, fear, relief.

For weeks, Darran just existed. Shock had set in and he was in total denial about what had happened. He was suffering so much mentally and physically, my heart broke seeing him go through this. He had lost so much weight, he was emaciated. So fragile. It was decided that he would be transferred to St Lawrence Hospital in Chepstow, where he spent a month undergoing skin grafting. He was then transferred back to Neath Hospital for recovery after all the surgeries he had had. He was such a brave person; I just don't know where he got the strength from. I felt helpless, all I could do was pray. These types of accidents always happen to someone else, you never think that they will happen to you.

Eventually, after months and months of treatment and skin grafts, Darran came home. Life would never be the same again. He had to get used to using a wheelchair and would become so frustrated trying to do things with one arm and leg. But he fought and with every frustration, he got stronger. I, still to this day, am in awe of him.

I would often think about the dream and how my mother kept reassuring me that everything would be all right.

When I reflect, I believe that the dream was a forewarning that something bad was going to happen. Somehow I had to focus now on the fact that my mother had offered me comfort. I kept thinking about her words, trying to reassure myself.

I went from being an ordinary housewife and mother to being a carer in such a short space of time. It's not something I thought about at the time, but when I think about how Darran and I adapted to such a traumatic experience, I now realise how we as humans can overcome such adversity and change in our lives.

Shortly after Darran came home from the hospital, Amy started nursery. Being such a sociable happy little girl, she loved every minute of school. Still, deep down I had this nagging feeling that Amy was different. She was so small in stature and was late learning to walk at 16 months, her speech was delayed. I so loved picking her up from nursery school, she would make me feel so happy seeing her beautiful, smiling face.

One day I picked Amy up from nursery and noticed she was unsteady on her feet and swaying to one side when she was walking. Concerned, I took her to the local surgery the same day and she saw a locum doctor whom she had never seen before. The doctor seemed intrigued and agreed with me, she felt there was more to Amy's situation, so she arranged a brain scan for the following day. It was a strange feeling, I felt both worried and relieved. Relieved in as much that someone was finally taking notice.

Amy had her brain scan and fortunately it was normal. However, a neurologist had decided to transfer Amy to the University Hospital of Wales in Cardiff for tests. Darran and I stayed at the hospital for two nights whilst the tests were done. Hair samples, skin biopsies and lots and lots of questions. Amy was oblivious to what was going on – she just kept smiling, unaware of how worried we were. Her gait was still unsteady, but the diagnosis of an ear infection had explained the balance problem. But I felt there was more news to come.

Three months later, the result came back. A name: 'Trichothiodystrophy'. We were told that the condition was very rare. The prognosis was vague because it is variable from one person to another. People with this condition are prone to infection and there is a high infant mortality rate. All this now made sense, as Amy was regularly hospitalised for infections and for the most part of her primary school years, her health was so delicate.

By the time we were given the diagnosis, I was now pregnant with our second child. We were referred for genetic counselling that revealed the one in four chance of this child having the same condition.

But this pregnancy felt so different. I had very little sickness, a good appetite and generally felt well. I knew our second child would not have the same condition. Ricky was born on November 8, 1988. He was beautiful, he weighed 8lb 9oz and it was clear he did not have the same condition as Amy. Amy adored her new baby brother and loved to help me bathe and dress him. He was such a bonny, beautiful baby.

Amy loved primary school and was so sociable. One day a poet called Adrian Mitchell was invited to the school to talk to the children about poetry. Amy's teacher at the time said that he had been very impressed with Amy's lovely smile and personality.

A few years later, Darran and I had decided to go to the Dylan Thomas Centre in Swansea to have lunch. When we walked into the foyer, we saw a café which was also a library for visitors. As I stood there, I noticed a very large book entitled *Who Killed Dylan Thomas?* and felt drawn to it. As I walked over to it, I could see Adrian Mitchell on the front. Recognising the name, I picked it up, flicking through the pages I saw a poem called 'For Amy Prosser'. There was a magnetism that drew me to the book. We felt so proud and emotional that he had written such a beautiful poem about Amy. In fact, there is a copy of his book kept permanently in the Dylan Thomas Museum.

Those were tough years. Caring for Darran, Amy and Ricky was a full-time job. I always felt there wasn't enough of me to go around. Things became a lot easier when Darran passed his driving test. It meant he now had mobility and could also take us out on day trips. He also gave me support, as I did not drive. Most importantly, it gave Darran freedom and a sense of achievement. I felt so proud of him. It was a new lease of life. When a disabled person drives their car, their disability becomes invisible. It's a great confidence boost.

Planning for holidays could be stressful at times, as there were so many things to think about, such as wheelchair access and amenities. We had decided to go to Spain, as a friend of a friend owned an apartment in Palma. It was a lovely apartment, everything was suitable for Darran, which made life so much easier. Having gone with some relatives and a friend, we had support if we needed anything.

During our week stay, the weather was not the best. It rained a few times, so it was up to us to entertain ourselves with things such as playing cards or board games. I had decided to go out on my own to have a look around, I wondered if there were any charity shops in the area. Charity shops are my true addiction, I just love them. After a short walk, I stopped someone to ask if there were any charity shops in the vicinity. As it happened, there was. It was a charity shop for lions. I found it quite easily despite it being a little off the beaten track. It was full of the usual stuff, books, bric-á-brac, etc., but nothing was catching my eye. As most charity shop addicts know, we get to a point where we simply have to buy anything just to fill our eyes and the till. Walking over to a shelf, there was a small plaster bridge with a plastic frog glued to it. I picked it up and smiled thinking of my little frog I saved in my childhood. That was it, my one and only purchase. I left the shop with my new find wrapped in some tissue paper.

When I got back to the apartment, I placed my little frog on top of the television. Its tackiness made me smile.

Later that day, Tina, a friend of the family, asked me about my charity shop trip. "Where did you get the frog?" she asked, smiling at it. I explained about my disappointment in not finding a Ming vase so I had make do with Freddo.

"Yes," she said, "but were they making them in the shop?"

I looked at her, not really understanding what she meant.

"What do you mean, Tina?" I asked.

"Well, you know, can I get one made for my grandson?"

I was completely baffled as to what she was talking about.

"No," I replied, "there was only one of them."

"So how is your name on it?"

"What do mean, Tina?" She picked up the frog and turned it around. There on the back was the name Joselin. Spelt differently to my name but my name nevertheless. Everyone was amazed, including me. What were the chances of that? Again, more than coincidence? I believe that intuition can guide us to certain objects and places at times for a reason. The universe is vast but each and everything within it has its place. I believe this small souvenir was meant to connect to me.

Amy's health started to improve in her early teens. She managed to attend mainstream comprehensive school despite having learning disabilities. She received a lot of support, including a personal assistant to help her stay safe in school, as she was so tiny and vulnerable.

Ricky attended a local primary school and was in good health. He was a typical boy, he could be naughty, but he was always lovable and helpful.

Ordinary days could be stressful and I would suffer from migraines quite often. At this time, my dreams were uneventful, not anything as vivid as I had experienced previously.

We had just celebrated my gran's 80th birthday, but now her health was failing. Shortly after her birthday, she suffered a stroke, which left her severely debilitated. Unable to live independently, she moved into a nursing home which was near to our home. Visiting her several times a week, her personality would change daily. Sometimes she would be happy, and we saw hints of the person we had known and loved so much. Other days her behaviour was antisocial and aggressive. She passed away in 2000. I felt so lucky and privileged to have had her in my life. She was the most wonderful caring woman, her selflessness had taught me so much. I would miss her dreadfully, but I had no choice other than to immerse myself in my family life and caring role. It would distract me from the grief I felt. Life goes on.

Amy's 18th birthday was coming up and we as a family wanted Amy to have a great party to celebrate. We arranged for a marquee to be set up in the garden and ordered a huge birthday cake. We had bought Amy various Swansea city gifts, as she is Swans mad. Picking up odds and ends in Swansea the day before the party, I felt an overwhelming yearning for my gran. If only she could see Amy at her party, she would have been so proud. I felt emotional. My gran always gave the children a 20-pound note for birthdays and Christmas, and I would marvel at Amy and Ricky's faces as they clutched the money tightly. Reminiscing, Darran and I decided to go for some lunch at our regular café. There was metal ramp for disabled customers to access the building. As I followed Darran, I looked down and saw something near my shoe. Picking it up, I could see it was a torn part of a 20-pound note, but more amazing than that, it was folded into the shape of a swan. If an origami expert had tried to make one, it couldn't have been better. This was my gran's way of speaking to me. I truly believe this. I have kept it in a small box with a photo of Amy ever since. For me, there is no doubt.

Darran had waited several years for compensation for his accident and was eventually awarded a large sum of money.

This enabled us to move from a small terraced house to a larger home (we had tried to find a bungalow locally but failed). We didn't want to move out of the area, as Amy and Ricky were settled in their schools. So we decided to adapt to our new house.

Darran and I talked about having a swimming pool built because it would be so difficult for him to go on the beach in his wheelchair, let alone go in the sea. It would prove almost an impossibility for him, so we decided to have an indoor pool installed within a small extension. It was to be just big enough to exercise and enjoy with the children, we felt that compensation should mean just that and a pool would compensate us as a family.

Next thing we had to do was to find a builder. Darran attended a local football club and was approached by a builder who was involved in the running of the club. Eager for us to employ him for the job, he turned up at our home with home-made apple pie. He was full of smiles and it was easy to be taken in. I had the sense of uneasiness about him. He had done work locally and didn't seem to have any negative feedback, although we had not spoken to anyone who had employed him, it was difficult to assess the situation. I had no logical reason to refuse him the job as he chatted with Darran about football; however, all the while I felt an inner discord. A few weeks passed and we finally decided to go with the 'Apple Pie' builder, despite my feelings of uneasiness.

We were given a written price on the job undertaken. As work commenced, we were aware that the bills of quantities had not been given to us. This was important because it was a breakdown of what was included in the price of the job. We paid monthly instalments by banker's cheques and continued to ask for the bills of quantities on a weekly basis, but to no avail. There was always a fresh excuse for not providing it.

Eventually, the job was completed and we made the final payment. The job was lovely, everything we had hoped for. It should have been a wonderful fresh new start for us as a family. But I still felt that there was going to be a problem – I was right.

Two months later, the builder came to our home with a briefcase, looking very business-like. He made small talk whilst I was preparing tea as he handed Darran an envelope. On the front it said 'final account'. He left swiftly before Darran had time to open the envelope. It was a bill for £16,000 outstanding. I rang his quantity surveyor and he was adamant that we had more than paid for the job and advised us not to pay another penny. He also told us that the bills of quantities had been with the builder for months.

We decided to stick to our guns and not pay the extra money until we had the bills of quantities, and this seemed a perfectly rational request. Soon we would receive a solicitor's letter. The builder had put the business in his son's name and his son had declared himself unemployed. As a result of this, his son had applied for legal aid successfully and now planned on suing us.

My feelings had been right all along. The builder's plan had obviously been worked out in advance – so devious. What followed nearly pushed us over the edge. We had to get a solicitor and barrister, which was now adding to the bill. The barrister's advice was to make him an offer as it would cost us more money to defend ourselves in court. A no-win situation. We offered £7,000 and it was accepted. I felt angry.

A few months later, I saw the builder at a local bank. Without thinking, I walked over to him and told him that the money he had extracted from Darran was 'blood money', that two men had been killed alongside Darran and reminded him of how Darran had to deal with his injuries mentally and physically on a daily basis. I asked him how he would feel if his son had sustained the same injuries. He was cold and unresponsive. This was the true person, not the 'nicey' person delivering the home-made apple pie.

A few months passed and we started to regain some sort of normality after the stress of the ordeal with the builder. It was hard to believe that a person could be so driven by money but I felt that he would have his own life lesson and find out that money is not that important compared to other things in life. Some people have no conscience at all.

More time passed, but I would still think about the builder and his premeditated plan. One particular night, I'd gone to bed and fell into a deep sleep. I dreamt that the builder was being forced into a room. I didn't know by whom. He was afraid. Suddenly, I woke up and kept repeating that the builder had not paid value-added tax on our job. I said it over and over again. Darran calmed me down and I fell back to sleep.

When I woke up in the morning, I knew this had been a strong dream. This time I was going to act on it. I rang the Inland Revenue and explained that I believed this builder had not paid VAT on the work we had had done. This phone call was followed by a visit from an inspector from Her Majesty Revenue and Customs. Our building society book was taken as evidence of receipt of payments. This was a case of putting my feet up and seeing what happened next.

A few weeks went by and I was informed that the builder's accounts were now being investigated. The result was as I thought, he had evaded paying VAT on the work he had done for us. All monies would have to be paid up front within a limited time scale to stop his son going through court proceedings, as the business was now in his name. I felt a sense of justice.

I then wrote to the legal aid board informing them that they had in fact aided and abetted a fraudulent person who had not been prepared to pay his taxes. It gave me great pleasure to receive a letter back from them stating that the legal aid had been revoked, so the builder would have to pay the legal costs of his representation when he tried to sue us. I'm not a spiteful, vengeful person, but this gave me a glimpse of what can be achieved if you do listen to your inner voice.

***

I have no elaborate explanation for dreams or intuitive feelings. The subconscious remains a mystery. I believe that possibly, this area of the brain takes over at occasions and can help with problem-solving almost in a fast-track way. Ultimately, I believe intuition is a gift and spiritual tool that can protect us from people and situations that could potentially do us harm. In a lifetime, we can use this to guide us through the most difficult of times. The more open our thinking is, the more the universe responds, I believe. We are spiritual beings that have lost our way somehow. It has become apparent to me on my life journey that doing the right thing is always the hardest thing and that our conscience is a higher power. Doing the easy thing will in the long run create new problems. As a species, we get things wrong. Wealth and power are so valued in our time, but I believe one day that there will be a fairer society. I believe that there will be an Age of Conscience in the future that will truly cleanse our planet.

Darran and I had been through so much together that sometimes our relationship suffered. We would both shut off our emotions because our life together had depleted our energies – not talking to one another enough, taking each other for granted. Someone had suggested me having a weekend break to recharge my batteries. Somewhere in my mind, I had always wanted to meet my father. My gran had said he seemed a nice man when she met him, but now I didn't really know if he was still alive. I started to google his name and then came up with the idea of phoning directory enquiries to see if there were Barillots listed living in Loudun, France. I was given three numbers of people with that surname. Nervously, I rang the first but it was not him, but the second call, I just knew the minute the phone was answered that it was my father. Unfortunately, I couldn't speak French but I only mentioned my name and he got quite excited. He spoke broken English to me, saying he had never forgotten me. I felt cautious and noted he kept asking for me to visit him.

I discussed whether it would be feasible for us all to go visit my father but Darran felt that it would be best if I went on my own or with a friend. I understood that the journey would probably be very stressful for everyone, so it was agreed that I would ask a friend. Arrangements were made for Darran to have support while I was away. I had decided just to go to France for a long weekend, from Friday till Monday.

It was a huge wrench going away without my family, I did feel a tinge of guilt. I felt so nervous about it all – leaving Darran and the children, something I had never done before. But it was something I needed to do. My friend Suzanne and I flew to Nantes, then caught a train and bus to Loudun. The journey was pleasant, admiring the beautiful scenery, I found the French people very easy-going and helpful, as we struggled with the language. Eventually, we arrived at Loudun and booked into our hotel. It was nice, clean and comfortable, the owners were very hospitable and welcoming.

Having settled into the hotel, we decided to get a taxi to my father's studio apartment. Feeling tired after the journey, we just kept going on adrenaline. The taxi driver seemed to know my father and took us to his address within minutes. Getting out of the taxi, I felt a wave of apprehension. The front door opened and this petite man with fine features smiled at us. I embraced him, not sure of my own emotions. Was this normal? I really didn't know. We sat down and he started to say that he had never forgotten me. The occasion was overwhelming really. Scanning his features and hands, I saw facets of myself within him. I felt a great sadness that I had met him so late in life. What-ifs came to mind. Every time I asked him about my mother, he would change the subject. Maybe it would take for him a while to open up; after all, this was an overwhelming moment for him too.

However, after two days of his company, he remained a closed book. I was only in Loudun for the weekend, so there wasn't adequate time to get to know him in any great depth. I just wondered why he had distanced himself from me for such a long time. I felt angry at him but he would have never known it as I smiled and struggled to bridge the language barrier. He was quite elderly now and I could see that his health was failing. His other daughter from his first marriage was living in Toronto of all places, and she visited him quite regularly. My feeling was that he had some personal issues possibly linked to his army service. There was a great sadness in his eyes. He explained that his parents had owned land and farmed in Loudun, and showed me several medals he had received for his army service. I was shown a photograph of his two sisters, who looked so familiar to me.

The last night of my visit, I was awoken by a horrific dream. I was soaked in sweat. In the dream, there was blood and body parts everywhere, some covered with plastic sheeting. Then my next-door neighbour's daughter showed me a beating heart on a silver salver. I felt so emotional, I cried and cried. I got up from bed and started packing. All I could think about was home. I rang Darran as soon as I could to make sure everything was okay at home, but he assured me everything was fine. Another 24 hours and I would be home.

My friend and I decided to go and explore Loudun for the last time. It is the most beautiful atmospheric town and we visited Loudun tower which seemed to fill me with a strange feeling of familiarity. In fact, I felt an affinity with the whole town just as though I had been there before. Do we possibly carry memory in our DNA from our ancestors? A hush descended on the town in the afternoon, the busy streets would become desolate. Within two hours, it would be bustling again. Youths on mopeds, French women carrying their sweet little dogs everywhere, and the smell of freshly baked sweet patisserie filled the air. One shop fascinated me, a bookshop selling very valuable rare mediaeval books. The handwritten manuscripts with detailed hand-painted illustrations were amazing. It felt as though the town itself whispered secrets. We absorbed the local hospitality, drinking coffee and people watching.

Heading back, I decided to say goodbye to my father. I gazed into his eyes and knew I would never see him again. The moment was so awkward when he begged me to stay but all I wanted was to go home to my family. I said goodbye and tried not to look back, but I felt a grief for the father I had never had. I cried. He had never written to me or sent a birthday card when I was a child. I just wished that he had. The journey home was bittersweet.

Arriving home, Darran greeted me at the bus station, I thanked my friend for sharing the journey and giving me the support and strength to do it. From the minute I got in the car with Darran, everything felt so different between us. He seemed disinterested. I wondered if he had felt resentment about my going to France. I kept thinking about the dream I had had in Loudun. The image of the beating heart. I couldn't pinpoint what was wrong between us. I told Darran about all about meeting my father, I was so relieved to be home with my family.

A week or two passed and Darran had taken me to Neath to do my regular shopping. Dropping me off, I told him I would be about three hours. We said goodbye and I did my usual shopping trip, arriving home after lunch. When I started to talk to Darran, I just sensed that there was something wrong. I don't know why, but I looked at him straight in the eye and told him I had had him followed while I had gone shopping. It was a complete bluff. He looked at me and got defensive. "Why would you do that?" he asked. I thought of the dream, the beating heart ripped out. I now knew it was a dream of betrayal.

Suddenly, I mentioned the name of a woman who would come into the charity shop where I had volunteered for several years. It was her. I just knew it. Within ten minutes, he had admitted everything. He had been seeing her for a few weeks. I felt sick, totally and utterly betrayed. The pain was unbearable. We just stopped talking after that but I knew instinctively that Darran had been flattered by this woman. I confided in a neighbour and told her what had happened; shortly after, her daughter and I had a conversation. It was her I had seen in my dream holding the heart. She explained that she knew of this woman.

Those weeks were very painful to look back on but slowly, Darran and I started to realise what we had been through in our lives together and what we could lose. It's so important to work through problems when you love one another. Forgiveness is healing oneself. All human beings are flawed truly, we all make mistakes but to build on them is one of life's greatest challenges. Ultimately, we loved each other and Darran was so sorry. This experience brought us closer together but also made us appreciate each other so much more.

***

As time went on, Amy won several awards for her wonderful attitude to life, including one at the Child of Achievement Awards which was held at the London Hilton on Park Lane. Despite having learning disabilities, Amy had managed to go through mainstream school and had such a wonderful attitude to life. Sir John Major, the former Prime Minister, presented her award along with other much-deserving and inspirational young people. It was a poignant evening, as there were some posthumous awards. Just heartbreaking but also a reminder of how precious life is.

Ricky was doing well at school, particularly writing and sports. We were so proud of the way he would support Amy and was very protective of her. I was always conscious of how much attention Amy required and would try to give Ricky the best of my time too, though sometimes I couldn't help feel guilty for all the constant flow of hospital appointments in our lives.

It was summertime and I had been asked to go on a school trip to the local country manor house, Margam Park, just to help out with supervising Ricky – who was seven at the time – and his class. I really looked forward to being around Ricky. On the day, the weather was quite fine and we did all the usual activities, the nature trail, pond dipping and consuming packed lunches. All good fun. The children's excitement always made me smile. Every now and then, Ricky would glance at me, making me aware that my presence was spoiling his street cred and did his best to avoid me. I found this so funny. A squirrel had become a major distraction to the children at one point, so he sneakily held my hand for a few seconds.

Later on that afternoon, the teacher explained that we would finish the day off with a walk up to 'Capel Mair' – the ancient ruin on the hillside overlooking the park. We scaled the hill until eventually we got to the top. It was an amazing site, very atmospheric, slightly menacing.

I was in mid-sentence talking to the teacher when this feeling of darkness descended upon me, I just felt as if I was under some sort of siege. My mind was drained as I tried to collect my thoughts. Such bleakness, I felt despair. How could I feel perfectly fine one minute and total despair the next? I had never experienced anything like this before.

Travelling home on the coach, my mind was not my own. I was a positive person – what was happening to me? Ricky and I arrived home and received lots of questions from Darran, but I just desperately needed to find a corner and crawl into it. I went to the bedroom and closed the door, making an excuse that I had a migraine. Lying down, I felt empty. It was an effort to draw breath as Darran came to check on me. But I didn't want to talk, not to anyone. Such a feeling of hopelessness, all the problems I had overcome, I just couldn't explain why I was feeling this way.

I made an appointment to see the doctor the following day, which couldn't come quickly enough. Sitting in the GP's office, I talked to the doctor about the events leading up to this feeling I now had. For a month or two previously, I had been feeling a little out of sorts, just a little down. Someone had recommended St John's Wort as a great 'pick me up'. So I had taken a tablet every day for about a month.

"You are suffering from acute depression," said the doctor. "It can happen in a split second," he explained. "Stop taking the St John's Wort, as your brain has produced too much serotonin." Serotonin is a feel-good hormone, he explained, but too much can actually cause depression.

I took the first medication for two days but I had side-effects, nausea and feeling detached. Still desperate, I returned to the GP. This time he prescribed a different antidepressant. As hopeless as I felt, I took them out of sheer desperation. After a couple of days, I noticed a subtle difference. Within two weeks, I felt like myself again. The black cloud had lifted, but I will never forget that feeling, it was so incredibly awful. Depression is a haunting, isolating condition but to know that the right medication can treat it is such a great comfort. After about a year, I stopped the treatment altogether. People should always seek help for this debilitating condition and never try to just cope with it.

Being a volunteer at my local charity shop has been a great lifeline. Just getting out and keeping in touch with the community can be good for the soul. I have made wonderful friends in the 20 years I worked there. My friend Ann, who is an amazing person, has managed the shop for the duration, unpaid and sometimes unappreciated. So many individuals and causes have benefited from the money raised by the shop, it's an honour for me to be a part of such a wonderful scheme.

Sorting through people's possessions, particularly if a person has passed away, is a poignant reminder that we never truly own anything, we simply just borrow material things for a while. Arriving at the shop one morning, I headed up the stairs to the sorting room. The landing is always brimming with boxes of unsuitable, broken items, bound for the rubbish tip. As I passed the last box, I noticed a handbag and was instantly drawn to it. Reaching into the box, I pulled it out to examine it. It was made of vinyl, possibly 1960s or 1970s. It was quite weathered and plain but why did I feel a connection to it? I opened it and looked in the pockets, which were all empty, I placed it back in the refuse box. Still I felt there was something unusual about the bag.

Working through the morning, chatting and drinking tea, my mind kept wandering back to the bag. About one o'clock, Darran rang to say he was waiting outside to pick me up. I put my coat on, made my way across the landing and lifted the bag out of the box again. I lifted it to eye level and rotated it around slowly, examining it. Then something caught my eye. Right at the base of the bag, I could see a tiny circular zip. Trying to open the zip, I realised it was very stiff. Eventually, it opened to reveal secret compartment, I could see something inside. Reaching in, I found a small gold locket with a man and woman's photo, a gold wedding ring and a cameo brooch. I felt a wave of emotion, as these items had been obviously so treasured by the owner. I connected with these people in the photo. I had felt intuitively that there was something about the bag I just knew. Two hours later, it would have ended up down the rubbish tip.

Having worked in the charity shop for so many years, I have made some wonderful friends. One particular friend is Jean. Jean is a glamorous, real get-up-and-go person, and despite being in her 80s, she has the energy of a 25-year-old. About seven years ago, Jean came into the shop on a regular Thursday morning. As a few of us started to chat and listen to an entertaining story that Norma, a great friend, was telling, I picked up that Jean was not herself. Quietly, I called her aside to ask her if anything was wrong. She opened up and explained that she felt there was something in her breast. Asking if she had been to the doctor's, she explained she had for an examination but nothing had been picked up. Deep in my mind, I knew Jean was right, there was something. I advised her to go back and see another doctor. This she did and it was the same result again, nothing was found.

Jean's son is a GP doctor, so I wondered about him giving her an examination. By this time, a few weeks had passed and Jean despite being examined and reassured by her son still felt that something had been missed. My advice to her was that if something felt wrong, then it was wrong. A scan was arranged a week later. It revealed a mass deep within the breast. Again, intuition is vital. Jean also had this feeling, but it would have been so easy after those examinations to not have pursued her gut feeling. But challenging logic is what we all must do at times.

Jean had to have a mastectomy followed by chemotherapy and radiotherapy. Before her surgery, I bought her an amethyst angel from a crystal shop, it was so beautiful. She took this with her to the hospital at the time of her surgery and carried it with her when she had her treatments. Jean had showed concern prior to the chemotherapy about the fact she was going to lose her hair. This was totally understandable, as she had the most fabulous dyed black hair that only she could get away with at her age. So glamorous, her pink lipstick completed the look. Jean has such a love of life, holidaying several times a year, I just admired her energy. Before the treatments, I told her that she would be back fighting, fit to live a full life again.

She certainly has done that. Despite the chemotherapy, she never lost her hair and is still the same after seven years, cruising, jetting all over the world. She is remarkable.

The other day, she told me she had given an inspirational talk about her experience of breast cancer. Someone asked her in the audience what got her through the experience. Jean looked at me and said, "My friend Jocelyn. She was my guardian angel." I just felt so emotional when she said that to me. I look at her now all these years later and wonder what might have happened if she had not had that scan. She is such a positive person, she is an inspiration to me.

In 2005, Amy developed a pain in her upper leg. I took her to see the GP and we quickly discovered that one leg was longer than the other. After a brief examination, he explained that Amy might need a hip replacement. She was referred to an orthopaedic surgeon who promptly explained that he did not want to undertake the surgery because Amy was so small, which made it a more complex procedure. Amy was 20 years old but weighed three and a half stone and wore clothes designed for seven-year-olds.

Amy was then referred to another surgeon. He seemed very confident and explained that she would need a customised hip replacement due to her size. This was a lot to take in. There was something nagging in my mind. Was this surgeon the right person for the job? I wondered if a paediatric orthopaedic surgeon would be a better choice because of Amy's small frame. I decided to contact the paediatrician that Amy had seen for many years just to get his opinion. Although Amy was no longer in his care, he kindly agreed to see us in his private office. I'd always found him direct and valued his opinion. We discussed whether Amy should have the surgery by the second orthopaedic consultant. The paediatrician explained that it would be a challenging operation for any surgeon. At least the second surgeon was young and confident – but was he the best choice?

A few days later, the orthopaedic surgeon requested that Amy attend the hospital seminar to discuss her case with many other orthopaedic surgeons who had come from far and wide to see her. They would discuss the best way to approach the surgery. It seemed that the surgeon had made every effort to prepare for Amy's surgery. It was easy to believe Amy was in good hands, we were desperate because by this time, Amy was in a lot of pain and discomfort. Needs must, we decided Amy was to have the surgery by this surgeon.

Uneasiness is a feeling that sits in your soul. Life's problems and necessities can distract you from a gut feeling. Amy by now was in so much pain that the process became a matter of urgency. It took a few months for the custom implant to be made and it was a great relief when Amy was called for the pre-assessment. She had the usual blood tests and questions she had been through some years previously when she had an invasive surgery on her jaws. A fantastic maxillofacial surgeon realigned Amy's upper and lower jaws. It took Amy months to get over that surgery. The surgery was Amy's choice and the surgeon did a wonderful job. I had never felt uneasy about Amy having this procedure, so why was I feeling so uncomfortable about this hip surgery?

After the pre-assessment, we made our way back to the car. Suddenly, we could hear someone calling us. It was the orthopaedic surgeon. He explained that the company had sent the wrong-sized hip implant and it would have to be sent back. This would prolong Amy suffering for a few more weeks. Annoyed, we just had to let it go, we just had to be patient.

A number of weeks later, Amy was rescheduled for the hip surgery. The morning of the surgery, I felt on edge. Doubt filled my mind. Was I just being a normal mother worrying about her daughter? It is normal to worry. Amidst these feelings, I just wanted Amy to be rid of the awful pain she was in.

The time arrived and the hospital porter came to get Amy. I sat near the window in her hospital room. The guilt I felt for her having to go through this ate away at me. I gave her a kiss before she left, but I didn't want her to see me crying and getting upset. Darran went to the operating theatre with her. He was so emotional when he returned. All we could do was sit and wait.

Sitting in the room, looking at the empty bed, longing for Amy's return, I glanced up to the window. There I saw the scruffiest dove just sitting in the tree near the window. It seemed as if it almost sensed our vigil. We were told the surgery would take about two and a half hours. By now, four hours had passed. I felt there was a problem.

I stared at the dove, which had been there for the duration, giving me comfort. The door opened and the surgeon entered the room, looking flustered.

"Amy is okay, but there was a problem."

"Is she all right?" I asked.

"Yes," he replied.

I looked out of the window and saw the dove ruffle its feathers and fly away.

We waited and Amy was eventually brought back to us. She was drowsy but still managed to smile. We were so relieved to see her, but what had been the problem doing surgery?

Later, the surgeon came to see us. Nothing could prepare us for what he was about to say. He explained the wrong-sized hip replacement had been sent again and that he had to cut it down during surgery. I felt so angry with myself. I had gone against my intuition, why did I not trust my feelings? Too late now.

Darran and I felt so angry, why was the implant not checked? Why was it used? I couldn't believe what I was hearing. After all the so-called preparations, scans, seminar rooms, it was a total botched job.

Weeks later, a letter arrived from the manufacturers, it was an apology. It stated that a standard 38mm BHR femoral head had been supplied in lieu of the custom device.

The manufacturer had allowed this supplier to manufacture custom devices without sufficient controls to assure compliance with requirements.

We read it in disbelief! But this was the second time the wrong size had been sent. Who forced the surgeon to use it? Who should have checked it? Smokescreens are there to hide the truth.

As the months wore on, it became evident that Amy could not lift her leg properly due to the weight of the implant. I sought legal advice but unbelievably it was deemed as satisfactory by another orthopaedic surgeon, who then went on to say that it was not negligent. Basically, Amy could walk, so therefore that was the end of that. Yes, Amy could walk, but what were the long-term implications of this implant? Amazing that the consultant who wrote the report did so without ever examining Amy. All very strange indeed, considering people have examinations for straightforward whiplash claims. Maybe it was because he too worked for the NHS and the company who supplied the implant is a billion-dollar concern. So much awkward silence to lots of my questions, i.e., why was the implant not checked. This question has still never been answered. There are a myriad of cock-ups and cover-ups within the NHS; all said, it is still a great institution. However, there is a more dark side to it where employees are afraid to speak out.

All this said, Amy would have to live with the consequences. No apology would be adequate. Mistakes can't be helped, but incompetence is unforgivable. I recalled the meeting with the paediatrician. I knew I had gone against my inner voice. Why? Because I believe logic takes over. Despite the seminar with many experienced surgeons discussing Amy's case, despite the custom hip implant being ordered, it all went wrong. Logic presents a perfectly good case for decision-making, but sometimes we have to trust and listen to the voice from deep within. It's there for a reason.

***

As a family, we tried to do as much as we could as a normal family – holidays, meals out, day trips, etc. Often I found my stress levels would peak after a busy week. Being a full-time carer, I found that I needed to find a quiet corner at times. My mother had been an amazing artist; to this day, her work intrigues, inspires and touches me, beckoning me to be creative.

Art became a distraction from the stress and I started to paint regularly. I'd left school whilst doing A-level art studies, finding the course boring. It was less practical and more emphasis on the history of art. Art is something that can be practised without qualifications or certificates. Paintings would evolve from my imagination without any planning. I also loved doing collage. I had thousands of cuttings in black rubbish bags which on occasions I would tip out all over the floor. People had given me old postcards and books to work with. I also recycled my 'gone-wrong' paintings, reusing them in collage work, which was really cathartic.

Once I remember picking up an old book and opening it to reveal the image of a man's face. I was completely drawn to it and cut it out immediately. Foraging through the mass of cuttings on the floor, I found a piece of paper which had come from an encyclopaedia. I mounted the image of the man's features on the top of the second piece of paper. It harmonised. Abstract, but somehow both pieces of paper belonged. I added just a few more small pieces and within half an hour, the picture was complete. As an afterthought, I went back to the book to see who the man was. His name was Sadi Carnot. Googling him, I learnt that he was a French physicist who worked on the heat engine theory. I then found the book the second piece of paper had been cut from. It was a photo of heating rods. I now understood how the two had connected. Allowing free thought can help us make connections.

I exhibited my work in various galleries and it just gave some sort of identity amidst my caring role. My art is described as self-taught visionary, intuitive, outsider. Many of my works naturally evolve without any planning. Spontaneity and intuitive attitude have produced my best work. When I overly plan for a painting, it seldom works out. The assemblage work is different in as much as I marry seemingly unconnected objects together. Once I had an exhibition at the

Washington Gallery in Penarth and had so much help and encouragement from Maggie Knight, the gallery director. I really loved and admired Maggie's drive and fantastic ability to champion well-deserving causes and people she believed in. When she left the gallery to go and live in Australia, I felt sad. Maggie had given me a pincushion dolly for an assemblage. It had belonged to her grandmother, so I decided to place the doll in a box which I had made, along with two dice and some playing cards. When I was hanging the exhibition in the gallery, Maggie asked to look at the assemblage.

"Did you know my grandmother was a professional gambler?" I just smiled, I had no knowledge of the pincushion dolly other than it was Maggie's grandmother's. She bought the assemblage and its image was used in the *Vale Life Magazine* and also the invites for the exhibition. Art also connected me to other people and through this, I met one of my most dear friends, artist Therese James. We were both self-taught and had no formal training. She is the most wonderful friend and confidante, and has actually been on a lot of my intuitional journeys with me. Therese had read an article about my work in the *Artists & Illustrators* magazine and decided to contact me. We had a joint exhibition in Therese's local town of Llanelli in 2003. After this we became the best of friends. Her work always makes me smile and lifts my soul.

***

In 2006, Amy needed her other hip operated on. Revision was a no-go area for her first hip, as we were told that it could make the situation far worse for her. I was determined that the second hip replacement would be done properly. Having found the surgeon whom I trusted, we discussed Amy's second hip replacement. He explained the implant would be manufactured from the mould that was in a hospital in America. A young girl of Amy's size had had the same operation. I felt at ease with the surgeon.

It took a few months for the hospital to receive the implant, but eventually it arrived. A date was scheduled for surgery and they felt a sense of relief that she would soon be out of the discomfort and pain. The pain from the original hip, unfortunately, was another matter.

On the day of surgery, Amy laughed and joked – she has a wicked sense of humour – asking Darran if he would pick up a small bottle of wine for her after the surgery. Darran and I both walked with her over to the operating theatre, both of us giving her a huge hug and kiss. I felt quite calm.

After three hours in surgery, Amy arrived back in her room. Tired, she managed to say a few words and then my beautiful girl fell asleep. I felt so proud of her, this tiny person never complained.

Darran suggested we go home and have a quick lunch just to leave Amy rest and head back soon after, so we left her sleeping and drove home. The distance between the hospital and home was approximately 18 miles. Arriving home, Darran handed me the front door key and I put it in the lock. Suddenly, I felt cold. There was an overwhelming panic. It was paralysing. "Darran, quick, we need to go back to the hospital now!" Darran just stared at me.

"What for?"

"It's Amy. Darran, we have to get back for Amy, there's something wrong. Please, just get us there as quickly as you can," I begged.

I can't remember the journey; my mind was flooded with panic. We arrived at the hospital and I ran ahead of Darran, who was on the phone with his mother. We got to Amy's room. Amy was sleeping. I walked over to her and sat down. Why did I have this awful feeling? I watched Amy breathing. One breath. Gap. Another breath. Gap. The gaps seemed like an eternity. I just knew something was dreadfully wrong.

I ran to the nurse's station and explained that I was worried about Amy's breathing. The nurse tried to dismiss me by saying that Amy was exhausted after surgery. But I knew she was wrong. I insisted on her calling for the doctor straight away. I felt so lightheaded, my mouth so dry, I could barely speak. Two minutes later, the doctor arrived with a woman. As I remember, she had an all-in-one jumpsuit on and was carrying a small case. My mind went into some sort of meltdown. Within minutes, I knew I had been right to panic. It felt as though everything was in slow motion.

Amy was administered adrenaline and was brought around suddenly. I remember her eyes looking glazed over. She was sitting up shivering. They wrapped her in a foil-type material. She was clearly in shock.

The woman in the jumpsuit walked over to me, looked into my eyes and touched my shoulder. She spoke quietly, "If you had been 20 minutes later, it would have been too late. You saved Amy's life."

I looked into her face. "Do you mean Amy could have died?"

"Yes," she replied. "Amy has overdosed on morphine."

I sat there trying to make sense of what had just happened. How could this have happened? Darran and I sobbed, it was all too much to take in.

The doctor explained that there had been no allowance made for Amy's body weight. At just three and a half stone, a morphine drip had been set up for Amy but the dosage was for a fully-grown adult. Amy had been told to press a button when she was in pain and the morphine would be released into her body. Amy had flooded her body with morphine and had overdosed.

I kept thinking of the feeling that I had had and how powerful it had been. What if I had not listened to my inner voice? Amy would have died. It just kept playing over and over in my mind. Human error again! I can't stress enough that if something feels wrong, it is wrong.

Amy made a good recovery after the surgery and despite the horrific incident with the morphine, I was thankful that the surgeon had done a good job on her hip. It left a bittersweet feeling in my mind. I felt Amy had been let down by incompetence again. But she was here, still alive, and that mattered more than anything. For me, I think the shock of what had happened left me reliving the moment for years.

In 2008, we decided to put our home up for sale and downsize. It seemed logical, as the upkeep would be easier for a smaller property. We already found a buyer for our house and had not found a suitable property for ourselves. Eventually, we found a nice property for sale in an area of Neath called Cadoxton. The estate agent selling ours was also selling this property. We liked the property, although it would need renovating, it seemed to tick all the boxes. After a second viewing, we put an offer in and it was accepted. Everything seemed fine and dandy. The day after our offered had been accepted, the estate agent called in for a quick chat. He slapped his hands together at one point, excited that he was going to make money from both sales. But a sudden feeling overwhelmed me and in a split second, I knew we just couldn't move to that property. Within half an hour, we had contacted the estate agent, who was quite annoyed and disappointed. But that was that. I just knew that that property was not meant for us. Having cold feet at the 11th hour, I set about looking on the property market again. I was not disappointed, a lovely bungalow had just come onto the market, and I hastily made an appointment for viewing.

The viewing proved that I had been right to pull out of the other sale. This property was so much better for us. As I entered the living area, I became emotional. I knew this was home. I have no idea what problems the other property would have presented in the long term but I just know, ultimately, an upturn proved be the right move.

Amy regularly attended a clinic at a local hospital. I would rather not say what department, as it might upset the family of the person involved.

The consultant Amy saw at this clinic was the most lovely, pure person – always smiling, never starchy or stand-offish as some consultants can be. Amy had seen him many times before and we were very fond of him. Good at his job, I knew Amy was in capable hands.

Writing about this is difficult for me. Amy had her usual appointment with the lovely consultant. As always, he was his usual courteous self. Smiling, he asked Amy about football (as she was a huge Swansea City fan), teasing her a little. I watched him laughing when suddenly a thought forced itself into my mind. "He needs a health check." I watched him while he examined Amy. His huge smile beaming at Amy, I asked myself why this thought had come into my head. He looked perfectly well. *Should I tell him my thoughts? Would he think I was mad?* Distracted by a knock on the door, Amy's consultation was over. I watched him smiling as a nurse queried him about another patient and then the lovely consultant disappeared down the corridor.

Six months later, Amy was sent a follow-up appointment. Arriving at the clinic, it was the most beautiful sunny day. We sat in our usual place in the waiting room.

Amy chatted away as we waited for her name to be called. Scanning the room, which had been redecorated, I noticed a photo up on the wall. Hospital waiting rooms are the most boring places, so anything that helps pass the time, even a few minutes, is greatly welcomed. I got up and walked over to the photo. A cold feeling rose through my body. It was the photo of the lovely consultant with the words: "Will be sadly missed by his friends." I felt so upset. A mixture of guilt and sadness affected me for a long time. I kept asking myself, *What if?* I found out that he had died of a sudden heart attack. He had no medical history of heart problems. Having spoken to another consultant who was a friend and colleague, it was apparent that he, along with everyone else, was in a state of shock. Once again I felt angry with myself. The consequences of not listening to intuition can be devastating. Could I have prevented his death? The question remains with me to this day.

Sometimes, my caring role would push my health to the brink – and occasionally it still can. In July 2009, I began to feel a bit rundown. On this particular day, I just started to have strange feelings. It was an intense feeling of *déjà vu* and also a strange, epic gastric-rising feeling in stomach. These feelings went on for hours. Eventually, feeling exhausted, I decided to go to bed and have an early night.

All I can remember after that was a paramedic looking into my eyes with a torch, asking me if I was all right. Dazed, I could see Darran crying in the corner of the bedroom with Ricky behind him. The next thing I remember was being in the hospital. The doctor explained that I had had what they believed to be a 'Grand Mal' seizure. I felt very emotional and confused as Darran sat at my side, holding my hand. He tried to reassure me that everything was going to be all right, but all I could think about was my family. Would I still be well enough to look after them?

The doctor explained that it might possibly have been a one-off event and I may never have another one. A month passed and I put the seizure behind me. However, I had started to have episodes of euphoria. Difficult to describe, it was a feeling of almost total enlightenment. Fleeting, I would have a glimpse of something quite incredible, almost divine, but the feeling would subside quickly, leaving me feeling flat and tired.

As these episodes started to increase, my GP made a referral to a neurologist. I had various tests – a brain scan, EEG, etc. Once the tests were completed, I attended a follow-up clinic. The neurologist explained that unfortunately there were no conclusive results, so I was going to be discharged. The consultant wished me a 'Merry Christmas' and so I left his room feeling the old familiar feeling.

I remember the snow on the ground and almost slipping as I made my way across the car park to Darran. He had waited in the car, as the ground was too slippery to use his wheelchair safely. As I travelled home, I knew there was a problem that had been missed by the neurologist – *but where should I go now?*

For two days I just waited, then guidance came. I felt I needed another MRI scan, but this time I wanted my neck included. I looked up a scanning unit in Cheltenham – it was private and I would have to pay. The second week in January, I travelled to Cheltenham with a letter of referral from my GP.

On the day, the scan took about 20 minutes. Afterwards, I waited a while as the neuroradiologist put the images on a disc and explained that the report would be sent to me within a week.

The report arrived a few days after the scan. I opened the envelope. This was a shortened version.

Head: There were a few minor abnormalities. Abnormally high signal in left posterior frontal white matter. There is no abnormality in the cerebral cortex or medical temporal lobe to act as an epileptogenic focus.

Cervical Spine: Multilevel degenerative change with reversal of normal cervical lordosis, spinal cord flattening.

Having read the report, I knew I would have to find a spinal consultant to explain it in detail. I found a great consultant who worked in Cardiff. Reading up on the website, I just knew he was going to help me. He was a neuro-orthopaedic surgeon who specialised in spinal surgery.

On meeting the consultant, I found him pleasant and forthright. He refused to look at the MRI disc or report until he had given me a full physical examination. He examined my fingers and tapped them individually. After a brief pause, he then explained that I had spinal cord compression. After this simple examination, he had come to this conclusion. He then put the disc in his computer and it became very clear that there was something very wrong with my neck. He explained three discs were almost in a state of collapse and that a simple fall or whiplash could result in paralysis. I just sat there. The other hospital had completely missed this. The consultant said he would have to operate on me as soon as possible but in the meantime for me to be very careful. Leaving the room, he told Darran to drive home safely.

As a carer, I just couldn't see how we were going to cope as a family. Needing an operation, I felt so guilty. When you're a carer, you don't really think of the impact your caring role will have long term. But years of looking after my family had taken its toll on my neck. I'd lifted Darran's wheelchair for 25 years, also lifting Amy in and out of the bath, carrying and lifting. As a carer, this is what we do.

Driving home, I remembered what the other consultant had said to me a few weeks previously, "Have a Merry

Christmas." He had missed a significant neurological problem. I also remember the snow on the ground that day and how I nearly slipped.

A few weeks passed and then the day of the surgery arrived. It took five hours. Three discs replaced and a titanium plate was fitted to reinforce my spine. I made a good recovery, but it would be a couple of months before I got back to my full caring role. I felt so grateful to the surgeon and his skill, which would enable me to continue my caring role. Some people we meet on our journey are like real-life angels, you feel immediately that you can trust them with your life.

Later I found out that spinal cord compression can cause seizures, so had this been the cause of the 'Grand Mal' seizure I'd had? Also, what were the strange feelings I was still having?

A familiar feeling returned, telling me to get a second opinion about the strange *déjà vu* feelings I was experiencing. In January 2011, I paid to see a neurologist in Cardiff. I explained the feelings and he said he would run some tests. We went through all my medical history, i.e., migraines. I would also wake up and see complicated spheres and patterns, which reminded me of a Spirograph set I had as a child.

There were also the epiphany-type feelings which sporadically gave me a deep understanding of why we are here. The moments were brief, they would slip away and I could not remember the information shown to me. It felt like a spiritual gate would open in a part of my brain for a second or two and then close. If roles were reversed and someone tried to explain these same feelings to me, I would have a problem believing in them. But these feelings *were* real and I *wasn't* crazy.

Again, I had all the usual tests and just waited patiently for the results. There was no doubt in my mind there was something wrong with me, but I felt such a great relief when the report arrived. It stated that my left temporal lobe had intricate epileptic-form abnormality.

A follow-up appointment with the neurologist gave a diagnosis of complex partial seizures. He said many of my symptoms were in keeping with this type of epilepsy.

The next step was a referral to a clinical psychologist to assess my cognitive function, as prolonged seizures can impact your memory and concentration, etc. I met the clinical psychologist for the first time at a Cardiff hospital and found her very pleasant. At the time, Ricky was buying his first home, which was local to us. The lady he was buying it from was working as a doctor at a Swansea hospital. I was really excited for him but also part of me was sad to know he was moving out and becoming 'a grown-up'.

Talking to the clinical psychologist at the hospital, I explained about my general health. After many questions regarding my wellbeing, I diverted the conversation to Ricky. I don't know why, but I began to talk about him buying his first home and I felt there was a link between the clinical psychologist and the lady Ricky was buying the house from. When I brought the lady's name into the conversation, the clinical psychologist just stared at me and said the woman was a very good friend of hers and they had shared digs together during their training. Each had gone off into different fields of medicine. Somehow I had felt their connection.

After this, I was able to talk at ease about past experiences. She didn't make me feel silly or delusional. It must have been a lot for her to take in.

After several consultations with her, she said she would send me a report on her findings. The report arrived after a few weeks. There was a lot to read and some of it I still don't really understand. The report summary included my general ability (53%) WTAR. Areas of weakness were for tasks demanding attention. Delayed memory was also noted.

The report summarised all the findings but to note there was nothing majorly wrong with me. However, one small line stood out in the report. She had described me as highly intuitive. I felt that finally my intuition was now being validated. It was an acknowledgement after all these years, which brought me inner peace.

After my clinical assessment, I was referred back to the neurologist. The plan now was a course of action to treat the epilepsy. By this time, I was having monthly seizures. Although they were disorientating, I somehow wanted to manage them without taking treatment. On the other hand, the neurologist was keen to start treatment, as he explained that the condition could get progressively worse.

I was prescribed Topamax and asked to consider taking them. But the 'red light' feeling was there again. Something was telling me not to take the tablets. In the small print of the packaging, there was a warning. Anyone with narrow angle glaucoma should not take the medication. My instinct was telling me to get my eyes checked out. I asked my GP to refer me to an eye specialist. An appointment was made for me to see the consultant in Cardiff. It was an evening appointment. I discussed my medical history with the consultant and explained about the Topamax which had been prescribed for the epilepsy. We chatted away as he examined my eyes and put drops in them. Now looking into my eyes, he started to look concerned. "Oh, you have occludable eyes."

Not understanding what he meant, he put more drops in each eye. He asked me to wait 20 minutes in the waiting room while he saw to another patient. He seemed edgy and uncomfortable. After the wait, I returned to his room. He examined my eyes, but I was still picking up that there was something wrong. He handed me some more drops and told me to take them as soon as I get home. He explained that a report would be sent to me within a few days. Travelling home, my vision was strange. In the dark, the streetlights were distorted, there were so many beams refracting off each light, creating a marigold flower affect. I felt unwell and nauseous.

Arriving home, I put the eye drops in and went straight to bed. On waking the following morning, my eyesight had returned to normal, much to my relief. The consultant rang that morning to enquire about my eyes and I explained that I had felt unwell the night before, but he just seemed to skim over my comments. The conversation was brief.

The report followed the consultation.

Basically, the eye consultant had noted that I had an occludable angle in my eyes, which theoretically in future could predispose to angle closure. He suggested I visit an optician annually. But I already had a regular optician who had never picked up on this eye condition. Also, my question about the Topamax was not answered. Was it safe for me to take? The report stated I didn't need iridotomies (a laser treatment to alleviate the possibility of narrow angle closure). I found this out when I googled the procedure. The consultation had been a waste of time.

I now looked like a very neurotic patient when I returned to my GP and asked for yet another referral for a second opinion. The GP was not happy, but despite me looking like a complete looney, he wrote another letter of referral. This time it was to see an eye specialist in Swansea. This is how intuition works: it's like trying to get over obstacles to reveal a truth. It's exhausting. A board game with real problems. But you have to go with it no matter what.

I attended an appointment with the second consultant. He was pleasant and once again I went through my medical history. I showed him the report from the previous consultant. There's also the question of the Topamax, and whether it was safe for me to take. After our discussion, the consultant examined my eyes carefully. I did explain to him what had happened when the other consultant had put eye drops in my eyes and how ill I felt afterwards. As I sat quietly, he wrote down numbers and examined my eyes carefully with a slit lamp. Once he had finished the examination, he sat a while and calculated the measurements of each eye. For ten minutes, there was complete silence in the room. Then he spoke,

"You have already had an episode of angle closure when the other consultant put drops in your eyes. All the symptoms are classic signs of acute angle closure – nausea and feeling unwell – you should have been sent straight to the hospital when this happened. Certain medications can build pressure within the eye. If you had taken the Topamax, on the 4th or 5th day, you would've gone permanently blind." I just sat there in silence.

He explained that when he started working in Swansea early on in his career, he would see at least one person blinded permanently a week because they had taken a medication not knowing they had this eye condition. Some over-the-counter medications for colds and flu contain phenylephrine hydrochloride. Some people like myself had no prior knowledge of narrow angle glaucoma. Despite my regular eye tests, this condition had not been picked up. Frightening. The next plan was for him to arrange iridotomies.

Lots of questions kept going through my mind. What if I had taken the medication? How would I have coped with being blind? How many people would just take medication without question? I felt relief, trusting that 'feeling' had saved me from a near-disaster again. My advice to anyone reading this is never give in to logic.

A few weeks later, I had iridotomies performed in both eyes. It's a fascinating procedure where the surgeon lasers a hole into the top of the iris at 12 o'clock. This hole then acts as a drainage, so if pressure builds up within that eye, the fluid can pass through the hole, acting as a drainage system. The procedure is completely quick and painless, but it can save people's eyesight. Also, the epilepsy treatment was now safe to take. I was grateful for the consultant's time and skill.

It's so important to challenge situations if they feel uncomfortable. Doing this, we sometimes have to stand alone in the midst of other people's opinions. Don't let the fear of being perceived as neurotic stop you from acting on your inner voice. My inner voice has proved its worth by now.

***

In April of 2011, we lost our wonderful dog, Dodo. He was 21. We had had Dodo from a pup – when Ricky was in nursery school – and he was so loveable and scruffy. This wonderful dog had seen all the trials and tribulations of our life journey together and we were so devastated after he died. The grief was overwhelming. I decided to look for another dog straight away. It wasn't about filling a gap, it was about giving another dog a loving home. A week later, we had a new addition to our family, Cue Poppy, a tiny Chihuahua with a big attitude. She was an adorable feisty little minx.

On one particular day, Poppy had been really quiet. She just lay in her bed, not really interested in anything. She was drinking and had eaten a little food. I had made arrangements for a lady to come from the Shaw Trust – a not-for-profit organisation that helps people with different disabilities. It was for Amy to fill in some forms for a placement in the Dog Trust, helping the resident dogs to socialise. Suddenly, I just decided to ring and cancel the appointment and take Poppy to the vets. I sensed an urgency.

We arrived at the vet's and Poppy saw a great vet. After a few minutes, he declared that Poppy's sugar levels were dangerously low. He gave her some Manuka honey and explained that she would have died without the sugar boost. This was a common occurrence in tiny young dogs, so I would have to be aware of this. Again, why did I go to the vet's in such a hurry? I know why.

The physical pain I was now experiencing in my back would fluctuate and so I took all the usual painkillers on bad days. My caring role could be tough on occasions – being unwell is not an option.

Waking up one morning with usual back pain, I just felt intuitively that I had a gynaecological problem too. There were no major symptoms but I just felt that a lumbar MRI scan would reveal another concern.

Telling Darran about my thoughts, I didn't feel overly worried about anything. My GP had requested the lumber and sacral areas to be assessed because of a lower disc problem. After the scan, I was told that the results would be with my GP within ten days.

The nagging feeling was there when I walked into the doctor's room to get the results. The doctor was not my usual doctor but seemed nice enough. I explained that I had come for the results of the MRI scan. He looked at the computer screen and read the report out. Basically, there were intervertebral disc bulges at L4 to L5 and L5 to S1. Nothing too major, just general wear and tear.

"Is there anything else?" I asked.

"No," he replied. He explained what medications were available to cover the pain and printed out a prescription.

Leaving the surgery, I just felt uneasiness, which by now was familiar to me. Getting back in the car, I asked Darran to drive to Aberavon Beach just to buy an ice cream. We loved to go and sit on the seafront. We both just sat watching the tide bringing in its usual treasure. Shells, crabs, fish, showing us the natural cycle of life and death in all its beauty, a never-ending cycle.

I turned to Darran and asked to borrow his mobile phone.

"Who are you phoning?" he asked.

"I just need to ring the surgery to ask for a printout of the MRI report." The GP had missed something, I just knew it. During a simple phone call to the surgery, I explained to the receptionist that I wanted a printout of my MRI scan report. She assured me it wouldn't be a problem and I could pick it up in half an hour.

We finished our ice creams and drove back to the surgery. The receptionist handed me a small piece of paper. The report was dated July 27, 2010. All the information about my lumbar discs was as the GP had related. However, at the end of the report was something he had not told me, it read: "The uterus appears bulky and fluid can be seen within the endometrial cavity. This may well be physiological but it is recommended that a routine ultrasound be done for further assessment."

The doctor had failed to relate this information to me. When I raised the issue with my regular GP, he made a referral for me to have an ultrasound scan. For a few weeks, I put it all in the back of my mind and didn't feel really worried, I just needed to have the ultrasound scan to have a clear understanding of what was going on. Life continued to be stressful at times but somehow we always got over the problems life set out for us as a family.

An appointment arrived for the ultrasound and I attended the clinic. The radiologist gelled up my tummy and started the procedure. She took images and measurements as we chatted about the weather, holidays, etc. Afterwards, she explained that the images would have to be examined and it would take a few days for the results.

A week later, I sat in my GP's office and was told that there was a very large growth in my womb and that I would have to have surgery to determine what it was. Again, I didn't feel any panic.

Surgery was arranged and the growth was removed. The following report described it as a very large endometrial fundal fibroid identified as covering the whole cavity. A biopsy was taken at the same time. The result – a fibroid polyp, no further action required.

Again, what would have happened if I hadn't had asked for the printout of my lumbar MRI scan report? It makes me wonder how often mistakes are made within the NHS. There are great people working within the NHS but there will always be mistakes due to human error. We must question things and challenge if we feel dissatisfied.

***

One of my great hobbies is visiting charity shops. I am always looking for old books and random items for my artwork. One day, Darran and I decided to go to Swansea for shopping. I was on my usual route for what I called the charity shop run. I would normally meet Darran for a coffee after an hour charity shop-hunting.

However, this particular day was different. I reached the market square and was about to go to Oxfam, but something told me to bypass it and go up to the Kingsway area. I knew there was a charity shop there somewhere but wasn't sure of its exact location. Walking as quickly as I could, feeling a strong pull, I reached the Kingsway and turned right. After a few hundred yards, I came to two charity shops next door to each other. I rushed into the second shop first, feeling a sense of urgency, scouring for that something I had no idea what I was looking for. When I got to the glass case at the counter, I could see something in the corner right at the back. It looked like a type of chain. The assistant dug deep and managed to get it out for me to look at. There was a price tag of £7.99. When I felt it and looked at it, it just seemed so old. There was a type of crucifix and medal pendants on what appeared to be a rosary made from some type of bone. It looked extraordinary.

When I returned home, Darran sent some photos of the rosary to the Rosary Workshop, which is a company that makes rosaries from mouldings of ancient designs. On their site, they have an online museum and a 'Can You Identify This?' section. We submitted ours and they kindly displayed all the photos of our rosary on the site.

After a few weeks, a man gave a description of the rosary, which was called 'The Lord of Miracles'. It was 16th century.

A section of the crucifix had been worn away in prayer and contemplation. I always wonder about the generations of people that held and prayed with this rosary. How many people had been comforted by it? The rosary photos are still online to this day and it is one of my favourite finds. If it could speak, I wonder what stories it would tell.

***

Thinking back to several years before, Darran and I had taken Amy and Ricky to see the illusionist Derren Brown at the Grand Theatre, Swansea. We had front-row tickets. Ricky loved Derren's series on television, so getting to see him close up was very exciting.

As the show commenced, Derren asked the audience to stand up. He instructed everyone to take a coin and place it in one hand behind their backs. Then, asking the audience to put both hands in front, whoever had the coin in the opposite hand to the one he specified would be told to sit down. The 'right or left' game continued until eventually there were only four people left standing. I was one of them. Derren went on to explain that we were 'challengers' and could not be used as volunteers for the show. This was proven later when a man who had been described as one of the challengers stepped up on the stage and was briskly sent back to his seat with Derren stating, "I can't use you." Challenging might be in a person's personality but it can't really explain the intuitive feelings that come from deep within.

As time went by, I developed new symptoms as part of my epilepsy: jaw clicking, picking imaginary bits off my clothing. I would see the most amazing, almost mathematical, spheres when I woke up some nights. Strange forms in mid-air so real, I could almost touch them. They would disappear after a few seconds. I wondered how the human brain is able to manufacture such complicated and perfect forms. So beautiful and fascinating.

**

In 2013, Darran decided to get another tattoo. Amy already had two small tattoos, not anything too conspicuous.

Visiting the local tattoo parlour, Amy had decided to come with us. As Darran looked through the design catalogues, Amy asked if she could have another tattoo. We had discussed her first tattoo at lengths before she had it done, having explained to her that it would be permanent should she get bored with it. This didn't faze her and she was thrilled with the result.

It is important for Amy to have as normal a life as possible. Yes, she has learning disabilities and does have to be guided in decision-making, but there is a fine line between guiding and control. To me, it's important to allow freedom of choice as much as possible. Amy has missed out on so much in life, so if having a tattoo makes her happy and feel good, that's fine.

Darran booked a date for his tattoo and explained to the assistant that Amy was having one too. Darran and I had a matching tattoo several years previously. The design was two doves and the word 'Hope' which we had done on the back of our wrists. The dove had become a symbol of hope, certainly to us. Over the many years of problems, a dove would appear in times of greatest hardship. It's also become more than coincidence.

Amy had chosen the same tattoo of the doves – it was apt considering the many problems she has faced.

Later that day, after we arrived home, Darran took a phone call which left him a little bit puzzled. After a lengthy conversation, we ascertained that the tattoo parlour had been contacted by Channel 4. They were making a documentary about interesting stories about women and the reasons why they have certain tattoos. Amy had been invited to take part. At first, I was not really happy about it. The last thing I wanted to have was any negative attention drawn to Amy. But then having spoken to the producer, he explained that it would be done sensitively. It would highlight Amy's condition and the problems that Amy faces on a daily basis.

One of the most frustrating things for Amy to have to deal with is when people assume she is a child. This is easily done, I know, as she is so tiny. Wearing age-seven clothes and her elfin face completely betray her actual age.

I remember waiting outside the academy in Birmingham, Darran, myself and Amy looking forward to seeing the 'Happy Mondays'. Amy loved Bez and all his dancing antics. Waiting patiently for the doors to open, a small posse of bouncers started to look over at us, they were trying not to look conspicuous. After a bit of elbow-nudging, the largest of them coughed and started to swagger over to us. As he approached, I held Amy's ID card up to him. No words were spoken. I felt like Clint Eastwood in *Dirty Harry* as I watched the big bouncer walk away into the distance. We laughed so much afterwards.

Another time, we took Amy to see Freddie Starr's show in Swansea. Three older women were sitting in front of us when one commented loudly about how disgusting it was to bring a child to the show. I bit my tongue as I know that saying something in front of Amy would've upset her but I felt so angry. Also, there are so many restaurants that have kindly given Amy crayons and colouring books. We thank them all.

But we have tried to laugh, because let's face it, life has these moments where ignorance is bliss.

The documentary team came to film and again we were assured that the filming would be a positive presentation. After a few hours of filming interviews, we were happy with the way things had gone. Next was the showing of the documentary. Watching it, I felt that Amy's story was so touching. She is such a wonderful person and radiates so much positive energy, no matter what. The documentary revealed how brave and inspirational Amy is. Contrary to popular belief, people do not get paid for the stories, but Amy did have a free tattoo and boy, did she tell everyone.

A few months later, I found myself at the centre of attention. Out of the blue, I had a phone call from the organisers of Lloyds Pharmacy's Carer of the Year competition to tell me I was one of the four winners. Darran had nominated me. I was very nervous about it all. Held at a swish London hotel in Mayfair, I felt so honoured to have been chosen from the thousands of entries. As a carer, I can probably speak for many of us when I say we don't expect accolades or medals for what we do. Caring is not a career choice, it is motivated by love and loyalty. Carers' lives can be affected in so many different ways: physically, mentally, emotionally and financially. Most carers don't even know they have rights. But they do.

My memory went back to the previous year. I had been so stressed and tired. As a carer, it's difficult to admit things are getting harder. My caring role had been the same for 26 years. Lifting Darran's wheelchair, helping with Amy's needs – tending to them both as best I could.

Having had spinal surgery and been diagnosed with epilepsy had made a difference in my caring role. Amy received a handful of hours of support a week from the local authority but I felt it wasn't enough. She was spending so much time with me and Darran. As a young person, she needed her own interests and hobbies. I had never asked the authorities for respite, I felt it was wrong for Amy to be refused more support. I was told by one particular person that

Amy was already receiving an acceptable amount of support a week.

At my wit's end, I rang Carers Wales, hoping someone could give me advice. Having poured my heart out to a wonderful lady called Beth, she went on to explain to me that as a carer, I did have rights. The Carers Right Charter meant that basically the local authorities were obliged to cater for my needs – all I had to do was to say I simply couldn't cope as a carer. I was dumbfounded by this information.

I felt empowered and was determined to get the support that both Amy and I needed. I won. Amy was granted the extra hours that we had requested, which would enable her to have a life of her own, to pursue her own interests and hobbies. It also meant that Darran and I would spend some quality time together as a married couple.

The Lloyds Pharmacy Carers awards arrived and Darran, Amy, my mother-in-law and I travelled to London for the event. We met the other carers who had also been nominated. Their stories really touched me deeply; although different to mine, there was a connection between us all.

The itinerary of events for us carers included a visit to the Deputy Prime Minister's house where we were to have tea. Having split into groups, we had taxis to take us to the address. It felt quite surreal. We arrived at our destination and were greeted by security guards. Nick Clegg's personal assistant showed us into the sitting room, which was beautiful. I love art and spotted a great painting above the fireplace. It was a painting of a vintage thermal flask and a cup on a travel blanket.

Nick Clegg arrived after a short while and greeted everyone. He showed a genuine interest in everyone's personal stories and their caring roles. We drank tea and discussed different aspects of caring. I then asked him about the painting above the fireplace. He explained that he had personally picked it from the government collection of art. It was called 'Tea' by David Tindle. There was also another work in the same room which he had also selected at the same time. It was a very large photograph of a room in a government building in a war-torn country. The room was in disarray and there were bullet holes in the wall, with a chair and desk overturned on the floor. The image was powerful and haunting. I asked him what had drawn him to this image. He explained it was a poignant reminder of how a country can revolt against its government when its people are oppressed. His choice of photograph revealed to me a compassionate, deep thinker.

As the time went on, his personal assistant kept whispering to him, reminding him of other commitments in the schedule for that day. Nick completely ignored the promptings and took us all out on the balcony at the back of his house, where he explained that the London Marathon finish line was literally outside the sitting room window. Afterwards, I was interviewed for the national Welsh TV news. Considering I was so nervous, it went well and the interview was shown on TV the following day.

I found Nick Clegg to be a kind and compassionate gentleman who made us as carers feel valued.

When we arrived back at the hotel, all the carers had to go through a rehearsal with the newsreader Natasha Kaplinsky, who is so glamorous and beautiful. When she called my name, I nervously went up onto the stage. Seeing my stress, she asked what I was most troubled about. I explained it was the fear of walking out in front of so many people that evening. She reassured me that it would all be perfectly fine on the night: "Think about the difficulties you and your family have been through, this will be easy compared to that."

Those words made a huge impact on me and when she called my name later that evening, I felt relatively calm walking up on stage and I even remembered to thank Carers UK and Carers Wales for their support, whilst Esther Rantzen presented me with my award. It was such an emotional evening, listening to the other carers' stories, I felt we were all kindred spirits, different situations but same struggles.

I have been honoured and privileged to have been one of the faces of Carers UK and Carers Wales consistently for the past few years. It was a huge honour when Carers UK used my photo for their International Women's Day 2017 promotion. I felt emotional when I saw that photo. Chris Steele Perkins, a professional photographer, had been commissioned to take photos on behalf of Carers UK. As a result, he came to our home to take photos of us as a family and me in my caring role. During the night, I had suffered several seizures and felt so tired when he arrived in the morning to take photos. That particular photo I hated at the time but it also captured a stark truth. I have come to love it now and see it almost as a battle scar moment. When I look back on my 30 years of caring, the most important thing I have learnt is that talking helps. By talking about a problem, you are allowing someone else to listen, to share that problem. Carers UK and Carers Wales provide critically needed advice, which provides a lifeline to thousands of carers across the UK by offering support, advice and also a platform to air worries and concerns.

Lloyds Pharmacy gave us the most amazing time, and I was so humbled to have had the opportunity to be involved in the event. Amy loved meeting the celebrities, especially Christopher Biggins. She had laughed so many times at him in Porridge with Ronnie Barker.

Arriving home, it was back to normal. Ricky now had a little family of his own, a beautiful baby boy and partner. Amy had a new boyfriend. Life is constantly evolving and changing. Family is so important, to love and respect is really what I believe our life journey is about. Trying not to leave problems becomes more important than the way we treat each other. Becoming a grandparent to our beautiful little grandson brought me such happiness and a new perspective towards life.

***

The last week in March, I had a strong dream. In the dream, Amy was unsteady on her feet and kept falling. When I woke up, I just felt so anxious, it felt it was more than just an ordinary dream – that warning feeling again. I had dreamt that Amy was near our large dining table. The image was haunting.

On March 30th, Amy woke up feeling under the weather and had developed a burning passing water. She started to be unsteady on her feet by the dining table as I had seen in my dream. *Dèjá vu* kicked in as I watched her stagger across the living room. It was a re-enactment of my dream. My first thought was to ring the surgery and try to get an appointment. All the appointments had been taken but the doctor would ring me sometime in the day. Once I had put the phone down, I felt the panic feeling like I had before. Grabbing an overnight bag, I threw on some pyjamas and toiletries and told Darran to get the car ready.

"We have to take Amy to the hospital now, Darran."

"The hospital? Why?" Darran asked.

"I don't know, but we must go now."

It was around 11 o'clock in the morning. We rushed to the nearest accident and emergency department and explained Amy's symptoms, which by now were getting worse. Amy had become confused and emotional and also had a high temperature.

We were fast-tracked to a treatment room in A&E and had not had to wait in the waiting room. The fact that this happened made me realise that there was something serious going on. I just felt it.

The doctors asked lots of questions while Amy was examined. Blood and urine samples were taken. The worst was yet to come. After an hour or two, the result. It was sepsis. At the time I didn't know a lot about the condition, which was just as well, as the survival rates for it are very depressing. We were told that the source of the infection was still unknown. Amy was to be given antibiotics and transferred to a ward for assessment. It was a small room at the bottom of the corridor. By then, the source of the problem had been discovered as a urine infection.

Amy looked so tiny in the hospital bed, and was very confused and unsettled. There was a poster of a maple leaf on the wall above Amy's bed. I enquired about its significance and a nurse explained that it was to inform members of the staff that the patient was vulnerable and at high risk of falling.

A few hours passed and Amy became more delirious and was just not able to communicate. So many thoughts came into my head. I watched as Darran paced around the room, it was so distressing to see Amy like this.

There were monitors and drips everywhere. I just kept praying. There was no continuity of nursing care. Nurses would come and go – agency nurses, along with regular nurses, but all would move on quickly and we would see new faces almost every day.

Amy had now been in the hospital for four days and was showing no signs of improvement. Darran and I had been at Amy's side constantly for that time, sleeping on the hospital floor at night. We were feeling exhausted, so when the nurse told us to go home and just get a good night's sleep, we reluctantly took her advice, trying to rationalise the situation.

By the time we arrived home, we just crawled into bed, praying Amy would show some sort of improvement by the morning. We were so consumed by her condition, it was difficult to think straight. At 1 a.m., Darran's phone started to ring, we had been sleeping for about three hours. I could hear by the tone of Darran's voice that there was something wrong. Darran looked at me. "It's Amy. She's fallen out of bed." I couldn't understand how she could have fallen. There were sides on the bed and Amy was unconscious.

We arrived at the hospital within half an hour of the phone call. I just felt so upset and guilty for leaving her, nothing was making sense. A nurse told us that one side of the bed had been left down for Amy to get a drink on the bedside table and she had rolled out of bed.

But in her condition, Amy wasn't capable of giving herself a bloody drink. Amy was helpless, she had lost consciousness days before. Total incompetence yet again. The maple leaf poster obviously hadn't meant anything to the nurse who left the bedside down as Amy lay unconscious.

By Friday, Amy's condition had deteriorated. We were called into a room and told that Amy had kidney failure. Our beautiful Amy was losing the battle. We were devastated. So much worry, so much love for Amy. It was the worst nightmare. So many tears for our girl.

Saturday, the situation remained the same, but by now I was completely disillusioned with the standard of nursing care. There were some good nurses and I was grateful for them, but nothing was joined up. Amy's drip would be left unconnected for hours on end. Most of the time we were trying to chase up staff to connect drips and give medication. Hours would pass and we wouldn't see a single nurse.

By Easter Sunday, I felt broken. We could see Amy fading. She had not eaten for eight days. Again the drip was unconnected.

Suddenly, I got an overwhelming urge to go to the main desk. My mind was fired up. As I approached the desk, I saw three doctors standing there and overheard them talking, "I'll tell the parents we won't resuscitate her, she has a rare genetic condition." I could no longer contain myself.

"What?" I asked. "Are you talking about my daughter? You just drew a line through her name without even seeing her. I want Amy taken to intensive care now."

Walking away from the desk, I had a seizure. Darran and my friend Kathy, who is a qualified nurse, sat me down. Sipping a glass of water, I explained what I had heard. Now I could see the full picture. The staff had already given up on Amy. The small room at the end of the corridor. All of it so obvious now. Amy had been written off. But every person deserves the right to live, to be treated equally. Amy certainly did. The doctor whose comment I had heard came into Amy's room looking sheepish.

I held out the photo of Amy receiving an award for being an inspirational person. Just because Amy had a rare condition didn't mean she didn't deserve a fair chance of survival. This now became a battle. Another doctor came from intensive care. I took an instant dislike to her.

"Amy can receive the same level of care here she would have in intensive care."

"What rubbish!" Darran exclaimed.

"Amy has had a fall due to incompetence here on this ward, drips have been left unconnected. Is this the way you run the intensive care unit?" I asked.

Amy deserved better treatment than this. The woman doctor just looked cold and unresponsive. She left.

At that lowest point, hope walked into the room. It was a young doctor. Just looking at him, I could see kindness in him.

"We will take Amy to intensive care now and make her better." I will never forget those words. The moment was just overwhelming. We felt so emotional. I believed in him. We said goodbye to a great young locum doctor who was working over the Easter period. He had also been sensitive and kind to Amy.

In these dark times, there will always be people who bring light. These people are what make the world a better place. They dare to do the right thing.

The minute Amy was transferred to intensive care, I felt different. Within a short space of time, Amy was receiving 24-hour care. There was no comparison to the care she received from the previous ward. Amy was now having regular medication, and within a few days, I could see an improvement, although she was still very ill and confused, she was managing to eat small amounts of food and drink. But to add to her already huge problems, she tested positive for influenza B.

I made regular trips to the hospital chapel, lit many candles, said many prayers, got angry, swore a lot and lost my faith in whatever I believed in. But this was pain, the pain of wanting to see Amy well again. The love and support I had from family and friends were my strength.

Amy was now stable, but then the unthinkable happened. She had another fall, still in intensive care, there was no real explanation for what happened. I felt so disillusioned with Amy's care. Trying to focus on the positives was my main priority.

Amy's kidneys were now starting to function properly and slowly I could see the improvement. It was hard to believe that Amy had lost nine pounds in weight. Her already tiny body now emaciated.

Eventually, Amy was transferred to another ward, as antibiotics were used now for controlling infection, but she was still confused. She spent another two weeks in this ward and was looked after well. There were lots of visitors too. Amy being a big Swansea City fan had a visit from Lee Trundle, who had been fantastic to Amy over many years. He visited her several times over the years after her operations. This visit made Amy smile so much, I didn't want him to leave.

I often think about how the most vulnerable people in society are treated. From my experience, I believe that they can be treated less favourably than other people. Every year, 1,200 people with a learning disability die avoidably in the NHS. We as a family had a meeting with the hospital clinical director to ask questions about Amy's treatment; however, it became apparent that he had no real answers, just an apology. He added that the hospital had failed Amy. But sometimes an apology is not enough. As human beings, isn't it our duty to care for the most vulnerable people in society?

After two weeks of care in the ward, Amy was discharged. It was a miracle that she was still alive. The survival statistics for sepsis are not good, but being given decent, proper care was Amy's lifeline. She was still confused and on occasions she didn't know who we were. She would drink from an imaginary cup and repeat the words "I don't want this" thousands of times a day. Basically, Amy's symptoms were similar to someone with Alzheimer's. She couldn't walk, every other step she would trip over, her body was just so weak. It was heartbreaking to see as it went on for months. I just kept giving Amy round-the-clock care; I would do anything to make her better, just anything.

Physiotherapists came to the house three times a week to try to strengthen her arms and legs. In her mind, she was not there, it was the constant confusion that got to me the most. But I kept hope somewhere safe inside of me. Without this, we are lost.

Every night, I would sleep next to Amy's bed to watch over here and help her go to the toilet in the middle of the night. She was helpless. One night I crept into my bedroom to talk to Darran, it was around three in the morning and Amy had fallen asleep. As I just sat looking out of the bedroom window, I saw a rainbow cascade of light which was in the centre of the garden. It was approximately 10 feet away from the window. So beautiful, I watched this as it kept flowing like water and changing in colour. Then it started to fade away. I had never seen anything like it. There was no doubt that it was real and that I saw it. The vision brought me comfort. Having no explanation for what I saw, my mind has its own theories. I had felt at my lowest point, emotionally and physically.

Not wanting to give up hope, I had to be realistic. Amy's birthday arrived on 24th of May. Amy's nana kissed our birthday girl on the cheek. Amy just looked at her blankly. Brain damage seemed to be the obvious explanation. She kept lifting her hand to her mouth and repeating words and gestures.

Then one night, I put Amy to bed and just sat at the end of it, just watching her innocent little face sleeping. I wondered about life and its purpose. It's the bad stuff that defines us, makes us weaker or stronger. Poppy, our tiny Chihuahua cross, had always had a love/hate relationship with Amy. Poppy would only sit on Amy's lap if I was unavailable. She was a bit of a user when it came to creature comforts and treats. If Poppy sat on my lap and Amy went to smooth her, Poppy could be snappy. This night, Poppy was different. As I sat watching Amy, Poppy was scrambling, trying to get on the bed. This was not usual for her. Leaning over, I picked Poppy up and put her on the bed. She sat there watching Amy. When I got into the bed, I expected Poppy to cuddle up to me, but she just stayed at Amy's side. After I fell asleep, I woke occasionally and saw Poppy still awake sitting there, watching Amy. It was very strange.

By the morning, I was puzzled to see Poppy still in the same position. The fact that she had not come anywhere near me was a first. It was quite early in the morning, about 7.30, I did the usual thing, put the kettle on, got breakfast ready while Amy still slept. Walking back into the bedroom, I could see Amy was stirring under the quilt. As I opened the blinds wide, Amy sat up in the bed, she just looked so different.

"Daniel is having his teeth done in Cardiff, but I think he's telling lies. Mum, could you pass me the glass of orange juice?" I was in a state of shock. Daniel was Amy's friend whom she had known for many years. Amy had been unable to converse properly for months since the sepsis. I passed her the orange juice. The impossible had happened. She had come back to us. It was a miracle. I just cried and cried. Just seeing Amy's beautiful mind return made me feel alive again.

As the weeks wore on, I knew that her body had been severely weakened by the sepsis. Amy was so frail. She had such an unsteady gait that there was a high possibility of falling. There was a constant worry that Amy could end up in the hospital again.

Through all these awful months, I knew Amy was a fighter, showing a strength that was almost superhuman. I reflected on the dream leading up to the sepsis and the cascade of beautiful light that I saw when Amy first came home. The light was a divine presence I believe.

For all these hard months, people were so kind to us as a family. So many people prayed for Amy far and wide. Tough times bring out the best in people and I am so thankful to everyone who showed us such love and kindness.

***

Amy's mind, although forgetful, continued to improve slowly. She was thrilled when Kevin Johns came to visit her. Kevin does so much for charity and is well known for his radio shows, and his pantomime dames are the best. Lovely people giving their time, because time is so precious to everyone.

For about 18 months, I had experienced episodes of a high heart rate. Assuming it was stress in all probability, I was sent to the local hospital for tests. The result was that I had some plaque build-up in my aorta. The heart consultant told me not to be overly concerned and that she would see me in about five years' time.

So I was discharged and told to remind my GP nearer the time for the next appointment.

My intuition was there again. Scanning the internet, I found a consultant who specialised in heart rhythm. I felt an affinity with the consultant's face – I knew he was going to help me. I requested a referral by my GP and was sent an appointment in due course. Meeting the consultant, I felt completely at ease as I explained my symptoms. Basically, he explained that I had three choices: I could have medication, do nothing, or have an ablation. I opted for the ablation, instinctively.

In the meantime, I was given a letter to fast-track me through A&E should I get palpitations. I had no real idea what an ablation was, all I knew was that I needed one. There was a waiting list for the procedure.

A few weeks later, Darran and I went to a park which I regularly visited as a child. I loved to walk up the Cenotaph steps as a child and trace my fingers over the cold bronze panels. Somehow I always felt close to my mother when I walked around this park. The same old trees overseeing people's lives as they had done when I was a child. Trees are a beautiful connection to the past.

Later, we arrived home and Darran had made me a cup of tea. Suddenly, I felt my heart going into fast mode. I took my pulse – my heart rate was 174 BPM. Grabbing the letter, Darran took me to the local hospital. I was fast-tracked straight into the treatment area and had an ECG. My heart rate was now 252 BPM. The doctor decided to transfer me to another hospital by ambulance. It was a strange feeling being tended to by a paramedic. I was feeling calm despite the pounding in my chest.

"Blood pressure is fine, it's just your heart rate – it's still 220."

"Oh well, I'm in good hands," I replied.

Arriving at the hospital, I had to go to the toilet. I instinctively splashed cold water on my face and suddenly my heart started to slow down. Apparently, this is called a vagal manoeuvre. Cold water splashed on the face can sometimes stop palpitations.

Unfortunately, it did not take long for my heart rate to rise back up again. The doctor came to see me and suggested that I take a low dose of beta-blockers. This seemed to be the best option for the time being, as I just wouldn't be able to function if my heart rate continued going up all the time. Despite all this, nobody knew why my heart was racing. It was a case of treating a symptom, not the cause.

It was only a week or two before the appointment arrived for the ablation. Honestly, I felt relieved, I just wanted to solve the problem. I made arrangements for Amy to stay with a friend overnight and on the day of surgery. Arriving at the hospital, I was briefed about the procedure and was taken to the operating theatre. I felt quite calm and relaxed. Talking to the staff, who were really friendly, helped.

One particular male nurse said to me: "I've been reading about you, in the notes, you're psychic." I looked at him, puzzled by what he meant.

"Pardon, are you talking about me?"

"Yes," he replied.

"Well, I am not sure what it says in the notes but I would describe myself as intuitive."

"Can you give me an example of this, then?" he asked. So briefly I explained about Amy's morphine overdose. He, along with a few others, were amazed and entertained and intrigued.

Assuming the staff read the clinical psychologist report, it's hard to explain intuition. My belief is that Poppy had an intuition the night she sat at Amy's side. She sensed something that even I didn't. I think most people have had some sort of intuitive experience at some point in their lives.

Truthfully, I can't remember a lot about the procedure, as I slept for most of it. I woke up a few minutes before the end.

"We've nearly finished now, Jocelyn, two minutes and we will be done."

All in all, the procedure took about an hour.

The procedure was a success, as they managed to ablate the problem area of my heart causing the palpitations. I felt such a sense of relief that I had managed to get the problem treated. The consultant explained that my heart had an unusual anatomy and only the ablation could have solved the problem. So I had once again made the right decision to opt for the ablation.

***

I feel an instant connection to certain people on occasion. Recently, I decided to take the dogs to Aberavon Beach. Being near the sea always calms and soothes me. This particular day, the weather was so mild, the sky blue and the sun beaming, giving a huge energy boost for a mid-October day.

As I started to walk on the sand with Poppy and Pixie, my little rescue dog, a beautiful young girl was beckoning to me. Immediately, I felt a strong connection to her. Sometimes we meet people who are so pure that only love and light emanates from them. I knew this young girl was one of these people. She loved stroking Poppy, who was so enjoying the attention, while Pixie of a nervous disposition hid behind me.

Jordanna introduced herself and the two lovely friends alongside her. I sensed her vulnerability and her true inner strength at the same time. It was explained to me that that Jordanna had had a very rare form of encephalitis, caused through a mosquito bite in Egypt. Only 10 people in the world have had this particular type of encephalitis. She had spent seven months in hospital and been critically ill for a considerable time. This was her first day out after leaving hospital. I felt so much empathy for this young girl. As I listened, it became apparent that Jordanna's speech and motor skills had been affected by the illness. I could see the same spirit in her as Amy, a fearless positive attitude which would surely help her on her long road to recovery.

She looked at me intently, "You are psychic, me too." At first I didn't catch what she said, so I said pardon and she repeated the same thing again. When I looked into her eyes, I knew she was highly intuitive, I felt so connected to her. I just wanted to give her something, a small gift to make her first day out of hospital special. I looked down at my hand and had a rock crystal, '70s' design Scandinavian ring. I loved this ring and had had it for many years but wanted Jordanna to have it. Reluctantly, she took it and started to cry, bless her. She was so appreciative, I just felt an overwhelming warmth to this brave young woman. She asked if she could keep in touch with me, so I explained about Amy and that she could contact me through Amy's Facebook, providing it was okay with her mum and dad. I had a lovely hug from her and her friends, and as I walked away, she shouted, "Honesty, transparency," put her hand up to wave and said it again. I knew that somehow those words would have some relevance to me. She had given me a message.

I called back to her, "Forward without fear." We smiled at each other.

Later that day, I saw a family relative that I had not seen for 14 years in town. Darran and I had not spoken to her for this duration because of a family dispute. Making my way to the market, I pretended I had not seen her, then I thought of Jordanna and turned back. It was an awkward conversation but I felt so much better for confronting the past actions of this person. After the conversation, we hugged and felt so much better. Jordanna was right, 'honesty, transparency' ruled the day.

A few weeks had gone by when a message came through Amy's Facebook page.

Are you the lady that spoke to my daughter on the beach? If so, could you give me a ring on my mobile?

I rang immediately, it was Jordanna's dad, Darol. He explained it was her 18th birthday on the following Sunday and she wanted to invite me to her party at home. I felt so happy that she had thought of me despite all her ongoing problems.

I visited Jordanna the afternoon of her birthday and had given a huge hug and smile. She showed the beautiful silver chain her parents had bought for her to wear the crystal ring on around her neck. She kept touching the ring, and her mum, Bec, explained that she wore it all the time. For some reason, I felt Jordanna was artistic and I had decided to buy an elaborate adult drawing colouring book for her birthday. It was a random gift I know but it just felt right for her. Her mum then explained to me that Jordanna had had an apprenticeship with a tattoo parlour before she became ill but her hands now had a tremor, so she would have to overcome this by rehabilitation. The book could help to build her confidence, as she could practise colouring intricate patterns and forms. With such wonderful parents and family, she had the most important thing to aid her recovery, love.

A week or two later, Jordanna's dad contacted us to ask if Amy would like to meet 'Busted' in HMV in Cardiff. Darol was involved with the security at the record signing. We were so thrilled to break the news to Amy, she was so excited and to get to meet Jordanna the same night. We had a fantastic evening, Jordanna was so lovely to Amy, just looking at the two of these young women filled me with pride and emotion.

***

A few months later, I was doing my usual shift at my charity shop when I was introduced to a lovely lady called Hayley who had become a new volunteer. It was nice to have a new face amongst us. Over the weeks, Hayley became one of the gang, always warm and welcoming to customers and staff alike.

This particular morning, I arrived at the charity shop as usual. The usual gang was there and we decided to have a cup of tea and a quick chat before getting on with some work. I noticed Hayley, who was putting some items of bric-a-brac out on the shelves. I just felt something was not quite right about her. I walked over to her and asked her if she was okay. She looked at me with a puzzled expression, "Yes, why do you ask?" I looked at her and I just explained that I felt she was unwell. I think this unnerved her, as she didn't quite understand my feelings. She reassured me that she felt perfectly well, but I remained unconvinced. I confided in Ann that I felt there was something very wrong with Hayley. I couldn't fight the feeling I got, I just knew there something wrong with her.

At the end of the morning, we all said our usual goodbyes, I looked at Hayley. What was I picking up from her? She obviously thought I was a bit nutty for approaching her as I did, but I think I would have been unnerved if someone had done the same thing to me. I explained to Darran in the car on the way home about Hayley and my feelings.

The following week, I went to the charity shop and noticed Hayley wasn't there. I wondered if I had put her off coming by unnerving her possibly. I asked Ann where Hayley was and Ann went on to explain that she had rung Hayley's mobile number several times but couldn't get an answer.

The following week was exactly the same, no Hayley. I felt something was not right, but Ann didn't have her address, only her phone number. Again she had tried several times to contact Hayley but had given up in the end.

About a month had passed when I walked into the charity and was greeted by Hayley and her lovely smile. "Oh my word, Hayley, where on earth have you been?" She looked at me studiously. "I have a story to tell you," she replied.

On the day I had last seen her in the shop, she had accompanied a friend to the local hospital for an outpatient's appointment, early afternoon. While sitting in the waiting room, Hayley collapsed, having had a grand mal seizure. I asked if she had ever had one before, she replied no. But that was not the end of the story, only the beginning. She was rushed to Morriston hospital, where she was diagnosed with a burst ovarian cyst and septicaemia. She was put on a life-support machine for five days. This explained her not answering Ann's calls, but she had obviously had a close escape. Again I have no explanation of how intuition works, but trusting the feeling is paramount.

A few weeks ago, I went to my local town to look around the charity shops. I went into several shops and didn't make any purchases. The last shop, I again looked around and couldn't find anything that caught my eye. Heading out through the door, I felt a tinge of guilt for not making a donation despite not buying anything. But then this thought came into my head. If I were to make a donation, it would be too easy. I gave myself a task to believe that the universe will reveal an item in the shop that will be of a special significance to me and to simply believe that this is possible.

I walked over to a small tray of pictures and picture frames. I flicked through the images and could see a piece of hardboard about five inches by four inches facing down. To get to it, I had to remove several frames. As I managed to grip it and turn it over, I felt completely overwhelmed. On the front of this piece of hardboard, there was a Japanese mask made of a resin composite. This was the answer to myself and the task I had set. The mask was an identical match to a beautiful bolo necklace pendant I have worn for over ten years. I had bought the original necklace at a charity shop and although a little grotesque, I loved the design. The universe led me back to that area in the shop. If I had simply made a donation, I would never have found it. And that is intuition.

Recently, I woke up feeling a little emotional and the fact it was Mother's Day, I think life can be overwhelming at times and I think Mother's Day is such a reflective day. Later, this particular evening, Darran and I watched television until about midnight. Turning the television off, I just felt like getting some fresh air. It was a beautiful starry night, such a clear sky. I made coffee and grabbed a large pillar candle, lit it and placed it in front of the large Buddha in the corner of the garden. I got the iPad and decided to play some music. It was an amazing song by Emeli Sandè called 'Breathing Underwater'. 'Breathing Underwater' reminds me of where we all come from – our mothers' wombs. I started to think of a lovely lady who was in London with her daughter while her daughter had had to have major surgery. I sent her a message through Facebook and told her I was thinking of her and her daughter. I thought about a little boy with Amy's condition who had been in intensive care for months, knowing his mum was alongside him. I was thinking of how hard life is, seeing our loved ones suffer and the special bond between mother and child. My mind asked why there was so much suffering in the world. I felt an overwhelming empathy. As I stood looking at the stars, I felt at one with the universe as though it was giving some comfort. I had goosebumps and felt a wondrous wave of peace wash over me, listening to the lyrics of the song added to the moment. Just as I looked up, I saw a shooting star. I slept so well that night, little did I know that the following night would be a huge marker in my life.

The following night seemed to be the usual. My dogs, Poppy and Pixie, were sleeping on the bed as they so love creature comforts. Poppy had developed nasal rhinitis over the past year or two, so I would give her a tiny amount of Manuka honey in the middle of the night to help clear her nose and throat. I normally kept a teaspoon and a jar of Manuka honey by the side of the bed. At about 3:30 pm, I woke up and heard her snuffling and reached for the honey and noted I felt unusually awake and fresh. Scooping a little honey on the edge of the spoon, Poppy started to lick enthusiastically. Suddenly, I started to see a flashing light in the bedroom which seemed to be coming from outside. I turned to the window and stood up. The sky was starry and clear like the previous night but as I stood there, the most amazing beam of light shone down into the garden, it was huge. At first I thought it might be a police helicopter chasing a car, but there was no sound at all, complete silence. The beam remained in place as it started to expand and retract. Then suddenly, it changed to a long cylindrical-shaped light, almost like a stratus-shaped cloud across the garden, it was moving in and out, and suddenly, smaller beams of light started to rotate in a circular motion, I tried to look to the sky to see what was responsible for this incredible light show. As I looked towards the patio doors, I could see blue lightning coming out of the ground. I was stunned. What was going on? I shook Darran to wake up, but just as he sat up in bed, the garden fell into complete darkness. I ran to the passageway to look out of the window to see if I could get a better look at the sky but there was nothing. I felt nervously excited about what I had seen. This display of light was definitely some sort of unknown science to me. I truly believe this. I did not feel afraid at any time but I did feel overwhelmed. The lights must have lasted about 20 to 25 seconds. The lower back of my head ached for about 20 minutes after, I could only compare that to the type of headache that I get before an electrical storm. This headache is normally at the front of my forehead, caused by a change in atmospherics. The headache after the lights was similar but at the back of my head, pulsating slightly. Somehow I found this whole experience comforting, maybe my soul searching regarding the universe may have been answered. To believe in a presence that we can connect with makes sense to me. This experience will stay with me always.

***

Remembering a day last year, I was in the car with Darran and I had become bored with Darran's choice of radio station Planet Rock. I turned the radio over to another station and exclaimed, "Let the universe speak now!" out loud…turning the control when we heard the words… "*Today is national Canada Day, tomorrow is World UFO day.*" Darran was stunned and his body covered in goosebumps as he continued driving the car. I just felt comfortable in the knowledge that the universe did speak to me. It spoke of my birthplace and of our true home, which is the universe. Synchronicities. We are all children of the universe.

Very recently, a close friend of mine, Edna, was wearing a new pair of glasses. I asked her where she had bought them from and she told me from a well-known chemist and the glasses were their own brand. I was compelled to take them off her and scrutinise them. There on the inside of the arms was a tiny writing. She looked a bit baffled as I tried to see what the word said. There it was, the word said Jocelyn. That was the name of the design. She looked completely in shock. I took it in my stride just accepting the synchronicity with ease.

I reflect on all the things I have written about here. These are only some of my experiences, not all of them. Darran says "Will anybody believe it?" He makes me laugh, because it's almost as if we have been written into a bad soap opera. Perhaps life is a bad soap opera.

One of the reasons I decided to write this book is to illustrate how intuition and open thinking can help us navigate through life and its problems. It has helped me steer through a maze of situations to positive outcomes. All I needed was to believe it was possible. To think openly opens many doors, I believe.

From my experience of intuition, it can create subtle or strong messages, almost like picking up a radio frequency. Dreams can also play a part in intuitive thinking. This can happen sometimes without us paying it much attention, as logic will very often push these feelings aside and it is only in hindsight that we realise that our intuition had tried to guide us. The mistakes that I have made in my life have clearly been the result of not listening to my inner voice. Most people would agree that they too have ignored their gut feeling at some point in their lives.

There are always going to be problems in people's lives, we know this, but maybe sometimes there is another way of dealing with them. Instead of automatically embracing logic, listen to the inner voice deep within. Let how you feel guide you through.

As for the future, I will be guided by how I feel in different situations. Animals rely on instinct for their survival – possibly we have lost that ability and rely too heavily on reason. Intuition, I believe, requires no explanation. It is a sure survival tool.

Time, space infinite,
Blood rushing through veins and heart,
Our immortal souls.
Jocelyn Prosser.